FOUR EXAMPLES

Katalog der Ausstellung / Catalogue of the Exhibition
Architekturgalerie Luzern
23. Juni bis 28. Juli 1996

Herausgeber / Editor: Edition Architekturgalerie Luzern

Architekturgalerie Luzern
Toni Häfliger, Heinz Wirz
Denkmalstraße 15, CH-6000 Luzern 6
Projektleitung Ausstellung / Exhibition Coordinator: Toni Häfliger
Mitarbeit Ausstellung / Exhibition Collaborator: Luca Deon
Projektleitung Katalog / Catalogue Coordinator: Heinz Wirz
Konzept Ausstellung und Katalog / Concept Exhibition and Catalogue: Patrick Devanthéry und Inès Lamunière
Gestaltung / Design: Vitamine, Dominique Emmenegger
Fotos / Photographs: Fausto Pluchinotta
Übersetzung ins Deutsche / Translation into German: Katja Anding, Berlin (Red. Ursula Suter)
Übersetzung ins Englische / Translation into English: Ingrid Taylor, München (Red. Barry Stanton)
Satz / Druck / Printing: Sticher Printing AG, Luzern

Library of Congress Cataloging-in-Publication Data
A CIP catalogue record for this book is available from the Library of Congress, Washington D.C., USA

Deutsche Bibliothek – CIP-Einheitsaufnahme
Devanthéry & Lamunière: four examples / mit einem Essay von Joseph Abram.
[Transl. French – German: Katja Anding. Transl. French – Engl.: Ingrid Taylor].
– Luzern: Ed. Architekturgalerie; Basel; Boston; Berlin: Birkhäuser, 1996
  Ausstellungskatalog
ISBN 3-7643-5435-6 (Basel...)
ISBN 0-8176-5435-6 (Boston)
NE: Devanthéry, Patrick [Ill.]; Abram, Joseph; Anding, Katja [Übers.]; Devanthéry and Lamunière

This work is subject to copyright. All rights reserved, whether the whole or part of the material is concerned, specifically the rights of translation, reprinting, re-use of illustrations, recitation, broadcasting, reproduction on microfilms or in other ways, and storage in data banks. For any kind of use permission of the copyright owner must be obtained.

© 1996 Edition Architekturgalerie Luzern, Rosenberghöhe 4, CH-6004 Luzern
© Alle Abbildungen: Devanthéry & Lamunière
Birkhäuser – Verlag für Architektur, P.O. Box 133, CH-4010 Basel, Switzerland
Printed on acid-free paper produced of chlorine-free pulp. TCF ∞
Printed in Switzerland
ISBN 3-7643-5435-6
ISBN 0-8176-5435-6

9 8 7 6 5 4 3 2 1

Edition Architekturgalerie Luzern

Birkhäuser Verlag
Basel • Boston • Berlin

FOUR EXAMPLES

INHALT

**6 SANFT ABSTRAHIERT /
ÜBERAUS KONKRET**
Joseph Abram

28 AUSSTELLEN
Patrick Devanthéry und Inès Lamunière

30 LAUSANNE
Aula der Technischen Hochschule

38 GRAND-SACONNEX
Grundschule und Freizeitzentrum

52 PULLY
Gymnasium von Chamblandes

66 CUGY
Villa Gringet

80 WERKVERZEICHNIS
1986–1996

CONTENTS

7 GENTLE ABSTRACTION / INFINITE CONCRETENESS
Joseph Abram

29 EXHIBITING
Patrick Devanthéry and Inès Lamunière

30 LAUSANNE
Main Lecture Hall of the Ecole Polytechnique

38 GRAND-SACONNEX
Primary School and Leisure Centre

52 PULLY
School of Chamblandes

66 CUGY
Gringet Residence

80 CATALOGUE OF PROJECTS AND BUILT WORKS
1986–1996

SANFT ABSTRAHIERT/
ÜBERAUS KONKRET

PATRICK DEVANTHÉRY UND INÈS LAMUNIÈRE: EINE DER WIRKLICHKEIT ZUGEWANDTE ARCHITEKTUR

«Wie kam mir die Schrift? So wie Vogelflaum an mein Fenster im Winter. Unverzüglich erhob sich im Kamin ein Kampf von glühenden Scheiten, der bis heute kein Ende fand.»

Seidenglänzende Städte des täglichen Blicks, eingefügt zwischen andere Städte, mit von uns selbst gezogenen Straßenzügen, unter dem Flügelschlag aus Blitzen, die auf unsere Aufmerksamkeiten antworten.

René Char, Die Bibliothek steht in Flammen[1]

Die Architektur von Patrick Devanthéry und Inès Lamunière sucht zwischen dem Wirklichen und Imaginären zu vermitteln, auf stille Weise die Grenze zwischen beiden aufzuheben oder vielmehr diese zu einer durchscheinenden, kaum mehr wahrnehmbaren Membran werden zu lassen. Zwischen einer Wirklichkeit, die immer bereits schon auf Veränderung hin zielt, und einem gedanklich Imaginären, das sich fortwährend von Wirklichkeit nährt, findet der Entwurf ein erstaunliches Gleichgewicht. Er bewegt sich wie zwischen zwei Meeren, eine seltsame Mischung aus Materie und Traum. Als Projektion auf den sich herauskristallisierenden Ort löst das Projekt die Entwicklungsgeschichte seiner Idee in einer Körperlichkeit auf, die aus Tausenden von unsichtbaren Fäden zusammengesponnen ist. Der Architektur erwächst ein Lustgewinn aus dieser Behandlung, und daraus, sich in der gleichzeitigen Vielfalt der alltäglichen Blicke zu verlieren. Produkt eines schlichten und gekonnten Arbeitsstils, weigert sie sich, narzißtisch als Zeugin ihrer eigenen Geschichte aufzutreten (mit der so verbreiteten Vorliebe für Entstehungsspuren). Sie verzichtet darauf, einem jeden mit ostentativen Zeichen zu bekunden, sie habe die Standortgegend berücksichtigt. Sie begnügt sich damit, es zu tun. Der Ort ist eine Wirklichkeit, die viel zu lebendig dafür ist, um nur dem Präsentationszweck zu dienen. Das Gebäude sollte sich ganz einfach dort befinden oder besser: dort verlieren. Es muß dabei nichts beweisen. Bedeutend ist nur seine Anwesenheit... seine Fähigkeit, eben da zu sein und nicht woanders.

1

Patrick Devanthéry und Inès Lamunière wenden sich gegen eine heute in vielen Zeitschriften propagierte Architektur der Beredtheit, die «dem Menschen eine Überfülle von Eindrücken aufzwingt», und mißtrauen jedem allzu deklamatorischen Ausdruck. Wozu sich lärmende Maschinerien ausdenken, wenn der erzeugte Raum dann nur die Zeichen des Raums zum Ausdruck bringt? Besser ist es, sich vor expressiven Ergüssen zu hüten, hinzustreben zu einer Architektur der diskreten Absichten, einer stummen oder fast stummen Architektur, die weniger «zum Sehen gemacht» ist als zum «Vergessen»[2]. Aber das Vergessen, um das es hier geht, ist keine

GENTLE ABSTRACTION / INFINITE CONCRETENESS

**ABSTRACTION DOUCE / INFINIE CONCRÉTUDE
UNE ARCHITECTURE ATTENTIVE AU RÉEL**

«Comment me vint l'écriture? Comme un duvet d'oiseau sur ma vitre, en hiver. Aussitôt s'éleva dans l'âtre une bataille de tisons qui n'a pas, encore à présent, pris fin.»
«Soyeuses villes du regard quotidien, insérées parmi d'autres villes, aux rues tracées par nous seuls, sous l'aile d'éclairs qui répondent à nos attentions.»
René Char, 1962

L'architecture de Patrick Devanthéry et Inès Lamunière propose une médiation entre le réel et l'imaginaire – une médiation tranquille visant à abolir une frontière, ou plutôt à en réduire l'emprise. Entre un réel imaginé pour être transformé et un imaginaire inlassablement nourri du réel, le projet trouve un équilibre improbable. Il navigue entre deux eaux comme une concrétion insolite de matière et de rêve. Projection sur le site d'un devenir coagulé, il annule la diachronie de sa conception dans une matérialité qu'il ajuste à des milliers de trames invisibles. L'architecture prend plaisir à être ainsi traitée, à s'effacer dans la complexité synchrone des regards quotidiens. Produit d'une élaboration simple et savante, elle refuse de s'afficher (avec cette complaisance si répandue pour les tracés) comme le témoin narcissique de sa propre histoire. Elle rejette les signes ostentatoires

PATRICK DEVANTHÉRY AND INÈS LAMUNIÈRE: AN ARCHITECTURE ATTENTIVE TO THE REAL

'How did writing come to me? Like a bird's down on my window in winter. At once, a battle of embers raged on the hearth, and has not yet ended.'

'Silky towns of the daily glance, inserted among other towns, their streets traced by us alone, brushed by the wings of lightning flashes which respond to our attention.'

René Char, 'The Library is on Fire' in The Archipelago of Words, 1962[1]

The architecture of Patrick Devanthéry and Inès Lamunière seeks to mediate between the real and the imaginary. Quietly abolishing the frontier between them, it seeks to reduce their hold to that of an almost imperceptible, diaphanous film. Between a reality imagined so that it can be transformed, and a theoretical, imaginary world tirelessly nourished by the real, the project finds an improbable equilibrium. It navigates between two seas like an unusual amalgam of matter and dream. Projected onto the site of a coagulated future, it annuls the diachronicity of its conception within a materiality that adjusts to thousands of invisible frames. Architecture takes pleasure in being treated in this way, or in being effaced in the synchronous complexity of everyday glances. Produced by a way of working which is both simple and knowing, it refuses to put itself on display (with the so frequently encountered predilection for traces of origin) as the narcissistic witness of its own history. It rejects the ostentatious signs which would guarantee to each, that it is respecting its setting. It contents itself with doing so. The site is a reality too vivid to be used as a prop. The building simply has to be there, or better still, to be lost there. It has nothing to prove. Only its presence matters... its faculty of being there, rather than elsewhere.

Denouncing the garrulous architecture which floods the reviews, and which 'imposes a surfeit of sensations on people', Patrick Devanthéry and Inès Lamunière mistrust over-literal demonstrations. What is the use of imagining noisy machinery, if the space produced gives form to nothing but signs of space? Better to avoid expressive effusions, and move towards an architecture discreet in its intentions? An architecture which is mute, or almost so, which would be presented less 'to be seen' than to be 'forgotten'[2]. But the forgetfulness we are concerned with here is not an effacement. If it implies a rejection of any a priori, fixed aesthetic, and the renouncement of the rhetorical procedures used to engender form. It nevertheless implies the search for an 'active' equilibrium capable of creating indestructible links between the components of the project and the concrete conditions on which it rests (economics, site, construction, etc.). It is about, on reflection, sublimating the logic of historical rationalism

Auslöschung. Zwar bedeutet es die Zurückweisung jeder a priori festgelegten Ästhetik und den Verzicht auf rhetorische Verfahren der Formerzeugung. Damit geht jedoch die Suche nach einem «aktiven» Gleichgewicht einher, das zwischen dem Entwurf in all seinen Bestandteilen und den konkreten Bedingungen, an die er gebunden ist (Wirtschaft, Standort, bauliche Realisierung), Bezüge unverbrüchlicher Art herstellen könnte. Es handelt sich, genau genommen, um eine Sublimierung der Logik des historischen Rationalismus durch ihre Beanspruchung für Dinge, die sich ihren Kontrollmöglichkeiten zu entziehen scheinen... Wie läßt sich, wird gefragt, hinausgehend über das, was als rationale Antwort auf ein gegebenes Bauprogramm (und die von ihm betroffene Wirklichkeit) gelten kann, eine besondere, klar erkennbare und jedem etwas bedeutende Poesie erschaffen? Mit Problemen dieser Art haben sich Patrick Devanthéry und Inès Lamunière schon seit ihren ersten Projekten auseinandergesetzt und sich im Laufe ihres besonderen Werdegangs (von Operationen auf Kleinstraumebene hin zur Restaurierung moderner Großbauten) ein kulturelles Handwerkszeug geschmiedet, das den souveränen Umgang mit solchen Fragen ermöglicht.

Exakte Ganzheiten

Wo liegen die heutigen Probleme der Architektur? Auf eine solche Frage gibt es, obgleich sie so naheliegt, keine einfache Antwort. Manche Architekten beenden ihre Karriere, ohne sich je den Schwierigkeiten gestellt zu haben, die ihrer Disziplin als Ganzes aus ihrem momentanen Stand erwachsen. Ihre Entwürfe bleiben an der Oberfläche der Dinge, ohne diese auch nur anzukratzen... Inès Lamunière und Patrick Devanthéry zeichnen sich dadurch aus, daß sie sehr früh den «Vogelflaum an ihrem Winterfenster» gesehen haben und seitdem, von einer Erfahrung zur nächsten, den nie endenden «Kampf von glühenden Scheiten» austragen... «Man kann ein Gedicht», sagt René Char, «nicht beginnen ohne ein Körnchen Irrtum über sich und die Welt, ohne einen Splitter von Unschuld bei den ersten Worten. Im Gedicht sollte jedes oder nahezu jedes Wort in seinem ursprünglichen Sinne gebraucht werden. Manche werden vieldeutig, wenn sie sich abheben. Andere sind erinnerungslos...»[3]. Den Ursprungswert der Worte wiederentdecken, alle Hüllen des Geläufigen ihnen abstreifend, dies könnte dem Ideal einer von jeder Rhetorik befreiten Architektur entsprechen: einer Architektur ohne Dogmen, die aus Respekt vor der Wirklichkeit ihre Mittel immer so einsetzt, als wären sie gerade erst neu erfunden.

Nach einem Studium an der Eidgenössischen Technischen Hochschule von Lausanne (wo Joseph Rykwert und Jacques Gubler zu ihren Professoren zählten)[4] und zwei am Schweizer Institut von Rom verbrachten Jahren (wo sie die Geometrie in den Werken von Pietro da Cortona, Bernini und Borromini erforschten)[5] gründeten Patrick Devanthéry und Inès Lamunière 1983 ihr Architekturbüro in Genf. Ihre ersten größeren, meistens für Wettbewer-

2

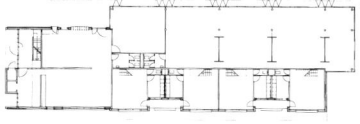

3

4

qui garantiraient à chacun qu'elle prend en compte le lieu. Elle se contente de le faire. Le site est un réel trop vivant pour devenir un faire-valoir. L'édifice doit simplement s'y trouver, ou mieux encore s'y perdre. Seule importe sa présence, sa faculté d'être ici, plutôt qu'ailleurs.

PD & IL se méfient des démonstrations. A quoi bon imaginer des machineries bruyantes, si l'espace produit ne met en forme que les signes de l'espace? Mieux vaut se garder des effusions expressives et tendre vers une architecture discrète dans ses intentions... Ceci suppose le rejet de toute esthétique fixée a priori et le renoncement aux procédés rhétoriques d'engendrement de la forme. Il s'agit de créer un équilibre actif capable de lier entre elles les composantes du projet et les conditions concrètes qui le portent (site, chantier...). Sublimer la logique du rationalisme en exacerbant ses exigences de contrôle. Fixer au-delà des réponses à un programme donné une poétique particulière, pour chacun signifiante... Comment identifier les problèmes contemporains? Certains architectes finiront leur carrière sans affronter ces difficultés inhérentes à leur discipline... La chance de PD & IL est d'avoir vu très tôt des «duvets d'oiseau sur leur vitre» et depuis, la «bataille dans l'âtre» n'a pas cessé... «On ne peut, dit encore René Char, commencer un poème sans une parcelle d'erreur sur soi et sur le monde, sans une paille d'innocence aux premiers mots.

by exacerbating its demands for control... How to create then, beyond the rational responses to a given program (and to the reality it transforms) a special, identifiable poetic quality which will be meaningful to all? These are the issues that Patrick Devanthéry and Inès Lamunière have confronted since their first projects, and it is in their own itinerary (from the mastering of micro-spaces to the restoration of large modern buildings) that they have forged the cultural means to accede to it.

Exact Totalities

How are we to identify the problems of contemporary architecture? However obvious the question, it has no simple answer. Some architects will finish their careers without having confronted those internal difficulties inherent to the very nature of their discipline. Their projects will slip over the surface of things without ever scratching it... It was the good fortune of Inès Lamunière and Patrick Devanthéry to have seen the 'bird's down on their window' very early on, and since then, from one experiment to the next, the 'battle on the hearth' has not ceased.... 'One cannot begin a poem,' says René Char, 'without a bit of error about oneself and about the world, without a scrap of innocence about the first words. In the poem each word, or almost each, must be used in its original sense. Some of them, detaching themselves, become multivalent. Others are amnesiac...'[3]. To discover the original value of words outside their gangue – such might be the ideal of an architecture stripped of all rhetoric. An architecture without dogmas in which, out of respect for the real, the means would be used as if for the first time.

After their studies at the Ecole Polytechnique Fédérale in Lausanne (where their teachers were Joseph Rykwert and Jacques Gubler)[4], and two years spent at the Swiss Institute in Rome (where they studied geometry in the works of Pietro da Cortona, Bernini and Borromini)[5], Patrick Devanthéry and Inès Lamunière opened their office in Geneva in 1983. Their first major projects, often produced for competitions (low-cost housing in Geneva [1985], collective housing in Aubonne [1987], hospital in Sierre [1987], hospital in Montreux [1987], residential housing in Basel (1, 2) [1988],...), reveal their attraction to the simplest formal solutions[6]. The geometry, always legible, is never imposed as an end in itself. It is inflected in response to the specific qualities of the site and the program, and it is this inflection which gives rise to the projects identity. The result is a relative complexity, which is not sought for its own sake. It arises naturally within the project, acquiring its own rights, and provided it respects local rules, it is willingly invited to express its own culture. As demonstrated by the building at Villars-Sainte-Croix (3, 4) [1986–1990], in this way architecture discovers its own necessity. Built at the periphery of Lausanne, at the articulation of different urban fabrics, this building describes the double heterogeneity of the

be erarbeiteten Entwürfe (Wohngebäude in Genf [1985] und Aubonne [1987], Krankenhaus in Siders [1987] sowie Montreux [1987], Wohnsiedlung in Basel (1, 2) [1988]...) lassen eine Vorliebe für Formallösungen schlichtester Art erkennen[6]. Die Geometrie drängt sich, wenn auch immer deutlich lesbar, nie als Selbstzweck in den Vordergrund. Sie beugt sich den jeweiligen Besonderheiten von Terrain und Bauprogramm, und gerade hierauf gründet die Identität des Entwurfs. Es entsteht eine relative Komplexität, die keineswegs künstlich gesucht ist. Sie macht sich auf selbstverständliche Weise im Entwurf wohnhaft – hat gewissermaßen dort Bürgerrecht –, und man läßt sie gerne zu Worte kommen, solange sie nur die Sitte zu wahren weiß. Wie das Gebäude von Villars-Sainte-Croix (1986–90) zeigt, erwächst der Architektur hieraus ihre Notwendigkeit. An der Peripherie von Lausanne gelegen, trägt das Bauwerk mittels der Ausbildung verschiedener Texturen die Spannung einer gleich zweifachen Heterogenität aus: Heterogenität sowohl seiner Nutzungen (Wohnungen, Betriebsbereich, Post) als auch der Orte, in deren Schwellenbereich es sich befindet (Wohn-, Industrie- und Landgegend). Der Baukörper ist kompakt, aber die Außenseiten verweisen auf die unterschiedlichen Innennutzungen sowie die je nach Orientierung andere äußere Umgebung (Holzfassade für die gegen das Dorf ausgerichteten Wohnungen, Glasfassade für die Post, die sich mit einem großen Portal zur Hauptstraße hin öffnet, industrielle Fassade mit metallenem Vordach für die Richtung Gewerbezone weisenden Betriebsräumlichkeiten). Wie Martin Steinmann und Philippe Gueissaz bereits bemerkten, läßt das Gebäude «sichtbar werden, was es trennt»[7]. Die Teilbereiche entwickeln eine jeweils eigene Sprache, die jedoch keine der mimetischen Anpassung ist, denn die verwendeten Ausdrucksmittel behalten immer ein Universelles. Aus dem Unausgeprägten einer Gegend von Häusern, Bauernhöfen und Gewerbehallen entpuppt sich durch die Architektur der Faden einer Identität.

Eine sehr ähnliche Form des Umgangs mit Komplexität ist beim Studentenwohnheim in Genf (5, 6) [1986–93] zu finden. Das Gebäude, auf einem Eckgrundstück gelegen, zwischen einem lärmreichen Boulevard und zwei ruhigeren Seitenstraßen, ist Beispiel für eine Verschmelzung von Bauprogramm und Ort zu einer «exakten» Ganzheit. Alle Bestandteile des Entwurfs wirken mit fast schon mechanischer Perfektion zusammen (erinnernd an das raffinierte Gefüge von Einzelteilchen im Innern einer Maschine). Das Wohnheim, das sich in seiner Höhe den benachbarten Bauten anpaßt, ist L-förmig angelegt und präsentiert vier Fassaden (paarweise sich entsprechend), die in ihrer Gestaltung durch Innen- und Außenraum gleichermaßen bestimmt sind. Zur ruhigen Seite hin: Eine elegante Fassade aus Aluminiumstreben und Glas spricht vom Repetitiven der dahinterliegenden Studentenzimmer und läßt durch ihre Transparenz deren gleichförmigen Rhythmus nach außen vorscheinen. Zur Seite des Straßenlärms: Eine Betonfassade mit Fensterbändern, die durch Glaspanele schildartig ver-

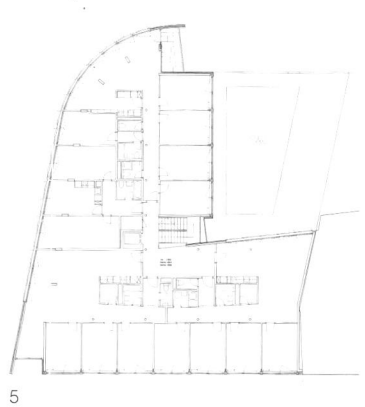

5

6

> Dans le poème, chaque mot ou presque doit être employé dans son sens originel...». Découvrir hors de leur gangue la valeur originelle des mots, tel pourrait être l'idéal d'une architecture sans dogmes, où par respect du réel, les moyens s'emploieraient comme s'ils étaient premiers (...).
> L'architecture de PD & IL tend vers la constitution de *totalités équilibrées*. Celles-ci ne reposent pas sur le recours à une force extérieure (qui fusionnerait les éléments), mais sur *l'exactitude* des dispositifs en présence. Elles supposent la limpidité des opérations d'assemblage. La construction se met au service d'une «expérience issue de l'insertion d'un programme dans la réalité d'un lieu». Et de cette insertion dans le réel s'envolent des essaims de significations, que l'architecture rassemble en quelques actes simples (...). Le projet pour un centre d'arts plastiques à Lausanne offre un bon exemple de totalité rigoureuse. Par son caractère «immatériel», il éclaire aux limites, la poétique des rapports «matière / espace» (...).
> PD & IL citent Max Bill, qui compare le béton «cette pierre que l'on forme» avec l'art qui est «l'expression matérialisée d'une conception de l'esprit». Cette remarque renvoie à une théorie de l'abstraction, qui a pris corps, pour Bill et pour plusieurs artistes de sa génération, durant les années 1930. Pour Arp (comme pour Van Doesburg), l'abstraction est un *art concret.* «Un tableau ou une sculpture, qui n'ont

program it houses (apartments, services, post office) and of qualities at the intersection of which it is situated (residential, industrial, and rural). Its volumetry is compact, but its outer faces reflect its internal uses and their position on the site (a wooden facade for the apartments facing the village; a glazed facade for the post office with a porch that opens onto the main street; an industrial facade with metal canopy for the services oriented towards the industrial zone). As Martin Steinmann and Phillippe Gueissaz note, the building 'makes visible what it separates'[7]. Each part develops its own language, but without mimetic references, as the vocabulary used remains universal. In this environment made up of houses, farms and industrial sheds, the architecture constructs from the banal, the semantic fabric of an identity.

The same management of complexity is seen in the students' housing in Geneva (5, 6) [1986–93]. Located on a corner site, between a noisy boulevard and two quiet, adjacent streets, this building provides an example of a concretion of program and place in an «exact» totality. All the components of the project are stabilized by a sort of mechanical perfection (evoking the sophisticated assemblage of parts that constitute a machine). Respecting the height of the neighbouring buildings, the L-shaped edifice offers four facades (as analogous pairs), whose configuration depends simultaneously on the inside and the outside. On the quiet side, an elegant grid of aluminum and glass expresses the repetition of the students' rooms and their static emergence upon the transparent membrane. On the noisy side, a concrete facade with strip windows (doubled with glass panels), translates the continuity of communal spaces (kitchen, living areas) and the dynamics of the boulevard. As Bruno Reichlin has remarked, this project develops the theme of 'forms in motion' experienced during the 1920's. Referring to precedents such as the Stummhaus by Bonatz in Düsseldorf (1922–24), the offices of ADGB by Max Taut in Berlin (1924–26), the Peterdorff department store by Erich Mendelsohn in Breslau (1928), or the Telschowhaus by the brothers Luckhardt in Berlin (1926–28), he explains how the 'Mendelsohnian horizontalism' is combined here with the 'expressionist verticalism'[8]. Reichlin also draws attention to the self-referential dimension of the project, which reveals the laws of its composition with 'the clarity of an anatomical écorché. He insists on the disengaged curved facade (which can be read like a 'dynamic mask' applied in the manner of a 'decorated shed'), and on the thematic redundancy of the noise attenuating 'scales' and of the 'saw-tooth motif' which emerges at the summit of the building.

This self-referential dimension seems fundamental, since the legibility it confers contributes to the formation of a 'balanced totality'. This totality, which seems to characterize the architecture of Patrick Devanthéry and Inès Lamunière, is not based on a recourse to some 'dramatic' external force (seeking to merge the elements of the project), but on the

doppelt sind, verweist auf die fließende Kontinuität der dort befindlichen Gemeinschaftsräume (Wohnküchen) und nimmt zugleich die Dynamik des Boulevards auf. Wie Bruno Reichlin nachweist, findet in diesem Entwurf der Gedanke der «Formen in Bewegung» seine Fortsetzung, mit dem in den 20er Jahren experimentiert wurde. Reichlin nennt als Vorläuferbauten unter anderem das Stummhaus von Paul Bonatz in Düsseldorf (1922–24), das Verwaltungsgebäude des Allgemeinen Deutschen Gewerkschaftsbunds von Max Taut in Berlin (1924–26), das Kaufhaus Peterdorff von Erich Mendelsohn in Breslau (1928) und das Telschowhaus der Brüder Luckhardt in Berlin (1926–28). Er zeigt auf, wie der «Mendelsohnsche Horizontalismus» sich hier mit dem «expressionistischen Vertikalismus» verbindet[8]. Ebenso macht er auf die selbstreferentielle Dimension dieser Architektur aufmerksam, die «mit der Deutlichkeit einer anatomischen Schnittzeichnung» die Regeln ihrer Komposition zu erkennen gibt. Er betont besonders die Loslösung der gekrümmten Fassade (die man wie eine «dynamische Maske» im Sinne eines «decorated shed» lesen kann) und die thematische Wiederholung der Lärmschutzschilder und des Sägeblattmotivs, die im obersten Gebäudeteil auftauchen.

Diese selbstreferentielle Dimension der Architektur erscheint mir wesentlich, denn sie schafft Einsichtigkeit und trägt damit zur Entstehung eines «ausgewogenen Ganzen» bei. Die Ganzheitlichkeit, die die Architektur von Patrick Devanthéry und Inès Lamunière zu kennzeichnen scheint, entspringt nicht einem abstrakt-äußerlichen «Dramaturgiewillen» (bestrebt, die einzelnen Elemente des Entwurfs zu verschmelzen), sondern dem «exakten» Umgang mit sämtlichem Vorhandenen. Sie impliziert feinfühlige Präzision bei den Operationen des Fügens, denn schließlich sind es diese, die dem Entwurf seinen inneren Zusammenhalt verleihen[9]. Die Entscheidungen im Technischen tragen zur Klarheit des Gesamten bei. Die Konstruktion wird niemals als autonome gedacht. Sie steht im Dienst «gestalterischer und funktionaler Ziele, die sich daraus entwickeln, daß ein gegebenes Bauprogramm in die Wirklichkeit und Substanz eines bestimmten Orts Einbettung findet»[10]. Eine solche Verankerung im Realen bewirkt, daß überall Partikel von Bedeutung aufwirbeln, die der Entwurf dann durch einige einfache Gesten bündelt. Das Studentenwohnheim von Genf greift so viel von latent in der Wirklichkeit Angelegtem auf und verarbeitet es mit derartiger Präzision, daß fast schon ein Schwebendes erreicht wird. Jeder Ausdruck erhält hier Vieldeutigkeit, so daß, trotz scheinbarer Schlichtheit, die unterschiedlichsten Lesarten möglich sind. Die Komplexität, aufscheinend hinter einer merkwürdig klassisch anmutenden Dreigliederung (Sockel, Körper, Krönung), macht dieses Gebäude zu einem außergewöhnlichen architektonischen Ereignis.

Der Entwurf eines Zentrums für zeitgenössische bildende Kunst in Lausanne (7,8) [1992] bietet ein weiteres Beispiel für jene Ganzheit der Strenge und zugleich Schwerelosigkeit[11]. Er wurde erarbeitet für einen Ideenwettbe-

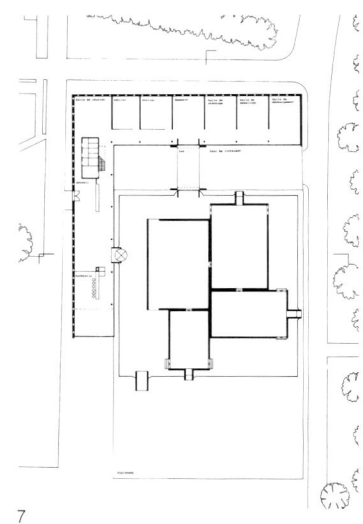

7

8

pas eu d'objet pour modèle, sont tout aussi concrets et sensuels qu'une feuille ou une pierre». Hélion définit l'abstraction dans un rapport renouvelé au réel. Dans la préface du catalogue de l'exposition «Thèse-Antithèse-Synthèse» (Lucerne, 1935), il écrit : «La supériorité de la nature est d'offrir le maximum de complexité de rapports». Les critiques verront bientôt dans sa peinture non pas «un symbole de la vie» mais «un morceau de vie» (...). Ce sont ces mêmes enjeux qui transparaissent aujourd'hui dans *l'architecture concrète* de PD & IL. Leurs réalisations récentes représentent un bond en avant dans cette conquête de la concrétude:
– L'Ecole-centre de loisirs du Grand-Saconnex montre une solidification de la *totalité*. Ce roc sombre gît au cœur de l'espace. Monolithe raffiné, il répercute son calme dans l'orbe du paysage. – Le gymnase de Chamblandes (au bord du Léman) se glisse entre une terrasse et des arbres, unifiant des éléments d'échelle et de nature différentes. Il absorbe le milieu qui l'entoure, transformant la vision pittoresque du paysage en une appréhension globale du volume vide qui colle au paysage. Sa façade développe un rythme régulier, fondé sur la subtilité des mesures et des matières. La résine verdâtre des ouvrants coagule la lumière et l'eau. Elle dialogue avec le verre et le rivage du lac (...). Toujours ajustée à son site, l'architecture de PD&IL est discrète, presque invisible...

Josef Abram

'exactitude' of the means used. It implies a lucidity in the operations of assembly, for it is these, finally, which ensure the mental cohesion of the project[9]. The technical decisions add to the clarity of the whole. The construction is never thought of as autonomous. It serves a 'plastic and functional experience resulting from the insertion of a program into the reality and substance of a place'[10]. From this insertion into the real, arises the swarms of meanings, which the project draws together in a few simple actions. The students' housing is adjusted to so many latent frames, and with such precision, that it seems suspended. Attaching a plurality of meanings to each act, it induces, through its simplicity, a complexity of readings which, subsumed in its unusual classical tripartition (base, body, crown), confers a scale of superb dignity.

The project for a centre of contemporary visual arts in Lausanne (7, 8) [1992] provides another example of this airy but rigorous totality[11]. In response to an ideas competition, which allowed the competitors to choose the site, the project is presented as the economic and functional juxtaposition (on a site already equipped for the Swiss National Exhibition of 1964), of an inflatable hall and an L-shaped building with a long screen-like enclosure[12]. An unusual object, without apparent qualities, the inflatable hall houses four exhibition rooms of different floor areas, joined side by side and opened onto a sky of white canvas. Around the four rooms, forming their negative, is a peripheral path, punctuated by large windows onto the park. The L-shaped building (which houses the offices, workshops and rooms for assembling exhibits) completes this 'exhibition machine', placed on the site like a zeppelin. A rational response to the problem posed, this project represents the archetype of a contemporary art centre. Through its 'immaterial' nature it illuminates to the limits, the poetics of relationships between 'matter/ space' in the architecture of Inès Lamunière and Patrick Devanthéry.

Endless Didactics

Involved in the combats of the architectural culture, Inès Lamunière and Patrick Devanthéry have become, through their projects, practitioners of a rare competence. Their path is that of a permanent apprenticeship. Their passion for history and for know-how led them naturally to the restoration of the modern heritage. 'To restore works of modernity is to re-learn their very complexity; a struggle between inculcated myths based on purity of form and a work within the interior of the plastic mass, or within the material and its method of fabrication'[13]. From the swimming pool at Bellerive-Plage to the lecture hall of the Ecole Polytechnique Fédérale of Lausanne, they have learned that two types of concrete are never the same, that creep in a building can be a kind of internal clock and an integral part of its identity, but above all that, the intimate analysis of a respected work, can become the condition for an architecture which is furtive, indiscernible. Is not the

werb, der den Teilnehmern die Wahl des Standorts freistellte. Inès Lamunière und Patrick Devanthéry schlugen vor, eine Traglufthalle und ein Gebäude in L-Form mit langgezogener Vorzäunung auf einem bereits für die Landesausstellung von 1964 erschlossenen Gelände nebeneinanderzustellen (eine Zweiteilung aus funktionalen und ökonomischen Gründen)¹². Die aufblasbare Halle, merkwürdiges Objekt ohne eigentliches Gesicht, beherbergt vier Ausstellungssäle unterschiedlichen Flächenausmaßes, die aneinandergruppiert sind und sich auf einen weißen Stoffhimmel hin öffnen. Um sie herum formt sich, als Negativ zu ihnen, ein Umgangsweg. Große Fenster gestatten hier den Blick auf den umliegenden Park. Das Gebäude in L-Form (das Büros, Ateliers und Montagehallen aufnimmt) ergänzt diesen «Ausstellungsapparat», der dem Gelände wie ein gelandeter Zeppelin aufsitzt. Insgesamt ist der Entwurf eine klare, rationale Antwort auf das gestellte Problem und kann für moderne Kunstzentren als ein Archetyp gelten. In seiner «Immaterialität» zeigt er eine Grenzform jener Poesie auf, die in der Architektur von Inès Lamunière und Patrick Devanthéry den Bezügen zwischen Materie und Raum entspringt.

Eine Lehre ohne Ende

Im Laufe ihrer Arbeit, ihrer ständigen Suche nach dem, was architektonische Kultur heute sein kann, sind Inès Lamunière und Patrick Devanthéry zu Praktikern von außergewöhnlicher Kompetenz geworden. Ihr Werdegang war der eines fortdauernden Lernens. Ihr leidenschaftliches Interesse für Architekturgeschichte und kühne Verfahrenstechnik führte sie wie selbstverständlich auf den Weg der Restaurierung modernen Kulturerbes. «Die Werke der Moderne restaurieren, heißt ihre Komplexität wiedererfassen; ein Kampf zwischen eingeimpften Mythen betreffend die Reinheit der Form und konkreter Arbeit an der plastischen Masse in ihrer Materialität und Machart»¹³. Im Unterwegs vom Strandbad Bellerive in Lausanne (9, 10) zur Aula der Universität von Lausanne haben Inès Lamunière und Patrick Devanthéry gelernt, daß Beton niemals gleich Beton ist, daß das Kriechen des Materials eine Art innere Uhr, d. h. wesentlicher Bestandteil der Identität eines Gebäudes sein kann, vor allem aber, daß die intime Analyse eines respektvoll behandelten Werks den Ausgangspunkt für einen architektonischen Eingriff bildet, der diskret ist und sich sozusagen voll zurücknimmt. Denn ist es nicht das höchste Ziel jeder Restaurierung, die auf profunde historische Kenntnisse gestützt ist, sich an der Oberfläche des geliebten Bauwerks zu verwischen? Architektonischer Eingriff meint hier Streben nach Durchsichtigkeit eines Films, sozusagen nach Virtualität. Der Entwurf muß das Gebäude seiner eigenen theoretischen Form wieder zuführen. Alle technischen Entscheidungen werden in Hinblick auf das Ziel getroffen, das Konkrete mit dem latenten Bild übereinstimmend zu machen, das die historischen Nachforschungen allmählich enthüllen. Wenn die Restaurierung verstanden wird als eine kreative Praxis

9

10

highest aim of restoration, when supported by real historical knowledge, to disappear from the surface of the well-loved work? The new project must therefore tend towards an architecture as thin as a membrane, almost virtual. It has to bring the building back into contact with the theoretical walls of its own mould. All the technical decisions then combine to make the task coincide with the latent image which is progressively revealed by the historical and technical investigation. If restoration is thought of as a creative practice (and not a passive and superficial one, as is often the case), all the energy of conception must be channelled towards the transformation of a very dense reality. The building itself supplies the information needed for the progressive formation of the abstract/concrete image towards which it must move. In this inversion of the relationships between the conceptual and the material, the project's object seems surreal in its concreteness. Whether the restoration concerns the carbonated concrete of the swimming pool at Bellerive-Plage (9, 10) [Marc Picard, 1934][14], or the pre-stressed concrete shell, deformed by creep, of the lecture hall of the Ecole Polytechnique Fédérale of Lausanne (Tschumi and Panchaud, 1962), to repair the substance of a work it is necessary to understand the logic of its design. For the shell of the lecture hall, calculated to allow a deflection of 6 cm, but demonstrating 33 cm of deflection in reality (taken up by the metal members of the glass facade), Patrick Devanthéry and Inès Lamunière incorporated the phenomenon of deformation itself in the solution. To restore meant for them: cutting away the upper parts of the vertical supports, allowing the shell to subside to its true deflection, and then repositioning the shell. 'This hybrid solution accommodates the additional load resulting from the re-finishing of highly carbonated and degraded concrete. A formwork system of 6 cm boards was reconstructed as a receptacle for the new layer of concrete. The concrete will be rough as before, without white paint, allowing the light to follow the complex traces of the formwork[15].

The knowledge accumulated through the restoration of modern buildings enhances (in return), the ordinary practice of design[16]. In terms of the scattered reality (program, site, construction,...) which constitutes a future edifice, an inverse strategy may be developed, which consists of identifying the project with the perfection of a latent image. If, in the practice of restoration, the real closes off the spatial definition by something absolutely concrete in the traditional practice, it opens on the contrary, to an infinity of possibilities. It is within this margin that the 'equilibrium of components' and the 'exact totality' that have been spoken of, take on their full meaning, as a premonition of the definitive character of the designed building. To this mastery of abstract/concrete relationships (sharpened by the practice of restoration), are added the scale/space relationships acquired through the 'microprojects'[17]. Small-scale interventions (creation of a duplex at Cully, 1986[18], a residential library at Bellevue, 1989[19], extension of a house at Carouge, 1990[20]) provide an ideal

(und nicht, wie häufig der Fall, als oberflächlicher und passiver Eingriff), werden sich alle Anstrengungen darauf ausrichten, eine Realität großer Dichte zu erreichen. Das Gebäude selbst liefert die Informationen, die zur allmählichen Hervorbringung jenes abstrakt/konkreten Bildes notwendig sind, auf das es dann wiederum hinstreben muß. Durch diese Art Umkehrung des üblichen Verhältnisses von Konzeption zu Material erscheint das Objekt des Entwurfs als ein in seiner Konkretheit surreales. Ob es sich nun um den zersetzten Beton des Strandbades Bellerive-Plage (Marc Piccard, 1934)[14] oder die durch Kriechen verformte Spannbetonschale der Aula in der Universität von Lausanne (Jean Tschumi und François Panchaud, 1962) handelt, immer ist, wenn die Substanz eines Gebäudes repariert werden soll, zunächst die Logik seiner Konzeption zu verstehen. Jeder Fall erfordert eine gesonderte Strategie, die auf einer Archäologie der historischen Konstruktionspraxis aufbaut. Bei der Aulaschale (gestützt von den Metallrahmen der Glasfassade), für die 6 cm als noch zulässige Durchbiegung kalkuliert waren, die tatsächlich aber 33 cm Durchhang aufwies, nahmen Patrick Devanthéry und Inès Lamunière das Phänomen der Deformation selbst in den Entwurf mit auf. Restaurieren hieß für sie: den oberen Teil der vertikalen Träger kappen, das Betonsegel insgesamt auf den Unterpunkt seines realen Durchhangs absenken und das Ganze erneut befestigen. «Diese hybride Lösung gestattet es, daß die durch Aufbesserung des stark zersetzten Betons entstandene Zusatzlast getragen werden kann. Eine Schalung mit 6 cm breiten Schalungsbrettern wurde konstruiert und Flüssigbeton eingegossen. Der Beton der Aula wird wie zuvor roh belassen, ohne Weißanstrich, so daß im Licht die Spuren der komplexen Schalungsweise hervortreten können»[15].

Die bei der Restaurierung moderner Bauten gesammelte Erfahrung wirkt auf die tägliche Entwurfsarbeit zurück und läßt sie strenger werden[16]. Denn gewissermaßen aus ihrer Umkehrung läßt sich angesichts der zerstreuten Wirklichkeit eines noch zukünftigen Gebäudes (Bauprogramm, Standort, Baustelle,...) eine Strategie entwickeln: dem Entwurf eine Stimmigkeit abverlangen, aufgrund derer er wie ein latent schon immer vorhandenes Bild erscheinen kann. Während beim Restaurieren das Wirkliche der räumlichen Definition die Schranke eines absoluten Konkreten setzt, öffnet es sie in der traditionellen Entwurfsarbeit hingegen auf ein Unendliches an Möglichkeiten. Erst wenn man die Arbeit Inès Lamunières und Patrick Devanthérys als eine zwischen diesen beiden Polen gespannte versteht, erhalten die zuvor verwendeten Wendungen wie «das Gleichgewicht der Komponenten» und «die exakte Ganzheit» ihren vollen Sinn. Sie beziehen sich auf die Art und Weise, wie hier den endgültigen Charakter des Gebäudes ahnend vorgespürt wird. Mit derselben Meisterschaft wie die Bezüge abstrakt/konkret (für die die Restaurationspraxis das Gespür schärft) werden Größendimension und Raum beherrscht, wozu die Arbeiten am «Mikro-Entwurf» beitrugen[17]. Die Eingriffe auf Kleinstraumebene (Gestaltung

laboratory for the test of space. The most remarkable project, for the precision of its approach, is undoubtedly the extension at Carouge (11, 12). A room and a bathroom had to be added to a house dating from the 1950's. Conceived as provisional (because of impending urban planning regulations), this addition takes the form of a wooden container, strained inside by a slightly curving partition, and opening as a full frame onto the garden. The box is inserted into the existent. It doesn't upset anything. The very detailed study of this modest space, and the aptness of the solutions adopted (wide window bay screened by blinds, loggia forming a frame, glazed full-height slit window which detaches from the partition...) give the project a true scale, and make of it, as Hans Frei has aptly written, a 'spatial poem'[21].

Following the Thread of the Real

In her inaugural lecture at the Ecole Polytechnique de Lausanne, Inès Lamunière quotes Max Bill who, in a text written in 1949 about Robert Maillart, compares concrete to 'that stone which we form' with art, which is 'the materialized expression of a mental concept'[22]. This comment of Max Bill's is not of circumstance. It leads to a fundamental reflection on abstraction, which came into being, for him and for several artists of his generation, in the mid-1930's. For Hans Arp, for example, (as for Van Doesburg, who initiated the expression), abstraction is a 'concrete art'. Every work of art is a concretion of creative thinking. 'A painting or a sculpture which haven't had an object as their model are just as concrete and sensuous as a leaf or a stone'. One must escape the dryness of abstract academism, which would be content to 'mirror life instead of creating it'[23]. Jean Hélion, for his part, tries to elucidate the implications of abstraction through a renewed relationship to the real. In the preface to the catalogue for the exhibition 'Thèse-Antithèse-Synthèse' (organized by Hans Erni in Lucerne in 1935)[24], he writes: 'The superiority of nature lies in offering the maximum complexity of relationships... On one hand, there are those who wander desperately around nature without daring to enter it, and on the other, those who through elementary structures, try to develop a language'[25]. Some critics will soon see in Jean Hélion's abstract painting not 'a symbol of life' but 'a piece of life', abstraction being not a comment on reality but a concretion of it[26].

The same preoccupation is discernible today in the work of Inès Lamunière and Patrick Devanthéry. They tend towards a concrete architecture which, 'like a leaf or a stone' is not a discourse on the real but a transformation of the real itself within an abstract practice. The most recent projects represent a major step forward in this conceptual conquest of the concreteness. The school and leisure centre at Grand-Saconnex (two programs housed in the same building) show how 'totality' has been consolidated. Cladded with slabs of quartzite of unequal width (placed at the bottom of the forms for the pre-

einer Duplex-Wohnung in Cully, 1986[18], einer Wohn-Bibliothek in Bellevue, 1989[19], Erweiterung eines Hauses in Carouge 1990[20]) sind ein ideales Training für kontrolliertes Raumdenken. Das aufgrund seiner Präzision sicherlich bemerkenswerteste Projekt ist die in Carouge vorgenommene Hauserweiterung (11, 12). Es ging darum, einem Wohnhaus der 50er Jahre ein weiteres Zimmer und ein Bad anzufügen. Nur provisorisch gedacht (da gerade stadtplanerische Neuverordnungen anstanden), ist der Erweiterungsbau ein Holz-Container, der im Innern durch eine leicht gekrümmte Wand aufgeteilt ist und sich Richtung Garten großflächig öffnet. Die «Box» fügt sich ins Vorhandene ein, sie stört in nichts. Die sehr durchdachte Gesamtanlage und die Überzeugungskraft jeder einzelnen Lösung (durch Jalousien geschützte Fensterwand; als Rahmen fungierende Loggia; über ganze Höhe sich durchziehender, verglaster Lichtschlitz, der die raumteilende Wand als plastisches Element hervorhebt) verleihen diesem kleinen Bau wahrhafte Größe oder machen ihn, wie Hans Frei sehr treffend bemerkte, zu einem «räumlichen Gedicht»[21].

An den Fäden der Wirklichkeit

Bei ihrer Antrittsvorlesung an der Eidgenössischen Technischen Hochschule von Lausanne zitierte Inès Lamunière Max Bill, der in einem Text von 1949 über Robert Maillart den Beton, «jenen Stein, den man formt», als Gleichnis heranzieht für eine Kunst des «materialisierten Ausdrucks einer geistigen Konzeption»[22]. Die Äußerung Max Bills ist keineswegs zufällig. Hinter ihr steht eine ganze Grundsatzdebatte um Abstraktion, in die er und andere Künstler seiner Generation ab etwa Mitte der 30er Jahre involviert waren. Hans Arp zum Beispiel betrachtete die Abstraktion als «konkrete Kunst» (und ebenso Van Doesburg, der diesen Ausdruck prägte). Jedes Kunstwerk, meinte er, sei Konkretion eines schöpferischen Gedankens. «Gemälde oder Skulpturen ohne realen Gegenstand als Modell sind ebenso konkret und sinnlich wie Blätter oder Steine.» Es gelte einem trockenen Akademismus zu entkommen, der sich damit begnüge «das Leben zu betrachten anstatt es zu schöpfen»[23]. Jean Hélion seinerseits versuchte, die Bedeutung der Abstraktion aus ihrer veränderten Sicht auf die Wirklichkeit zu begründen. Im Vorwort zum Katalog der Ausstellung «These – Antithese – Synthese» (die 1935 von Hans Erni in Luzern organisiert wurde)[24] schieb er: «Das Überwältigende der Natur liegt darin, daß sie ein Höchstmaß an komplexen Bezügen aufweist… Auf der einen Seite gibt es nun diejenigen, die verzweifelt um die Natur kreisen, ohne sich in sie hineinzuwagen, auf der anderen diejenigen, die, ausgehend von einigen elementaren Strukturen, eine neue Sprache zu entwickeln suchen»[25]. Wenig später sahen erste Kritiker in der abstrakten Malerei Jean Hélions nicht mehr «Symbol», sondern «Teilstück selbst des Lebens», erkennend, daß es sich hier keineswegs um Kommentar zur Realität, sondern um konkretes Umsetzen von ihr handelte[26].

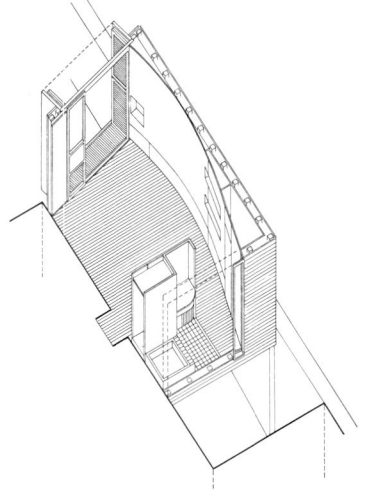

11

12

cast panels), this building appears as a dark mass. A large 'canopy beam' of pre-stressed concrete, gathers all the spaces (including the open-air hall through which the school and leisure centre are reached). It sets the large scale from one end of the project to the other. On the exterior, it defines the reception terrace as an intermediate space, framing it in relationship to the sky and the landscape below. Inside, it becomes a kind of light machine, recording the sun's course throughout the day by the repetition of its projected shadows (13, 14). The space is thus coloured by time. The flatness of the concrete and wood surfaces let the light flow freely. The classrooms in front open with large bays upon the neighbouring trees. Those placed at the back open onto the terrace where from one side to the other, a half-natural, half-urban landscape stretches. The edifice finds there its meaning. It has something of a stone about it. The choice of quartzite for the facades contributes to the abstract robustness of the whole. 'To take a material associated to the very idea, not so much of the school, but with teaching (a slate allows chalk and writing), is to postulate that necessity and technique form here a whole based on the means at hand, archaic perhaps, it became through weight, roughness and non-colour, an element of non-architecture; they are nothing but walls and boards… As for the concrete which is poured between two boards, it bears the mark of its fabrication, its robustness, its own destiny, as if turned upon itself[27]. This dark and tranquil rock rests in the heart of the space. A refined monolith, it spreads its calm beyond the site, into the encircling landscape.

Like the school at Grand-Saconnex, the extension of the school at Chamblandes (15, 16) [1992–96] faces the landscape[28]. Built on the edge of Lake Geneva, below two older buildings it supplements, this elegant bar is inserted between a terrace and trees. By its presence, it unifies elements of different scales and types. To the north, it acts at the end of the courtyard as a socle (or rather as the limit of the socle that it creates to the advantage of the existing building). Its slight emergence and its yellow-grey cladding of Saint-Triphon stone (of which the older buildings are constructed) confirm, from this side, its adherence to the base. To the south, it has a triple function. Through the wide opening of its porch, it frames the landscape of trees and water to form a deep tableau. Through its south facade, where wide bays alternate with narrower openings, it provides for a more continuous view on the lake. Through the platform which constitutes its roof, it transforms the picturesque scene into a contemporary vision, capturing at once and rebounding upon the horizontal surface of the terrace, the garden, the lake and the surrounding mountains. The building therefore, pushes back the boundaries of its field of action, accomplishing for the architecture, the spatial dream of certain artists of the 1930s. In a premonitory text on the 'composition of space', Wladyslaw Strzeminski and Katarzyna Kobro observe that sculpture knows no a priori limits. These emerge afterwards. For

Was heute in den Arbeiten von Inès Lamunière und Patrick Devanthéry aufscheint, sind sehr ähnliche Anliegen. Das Bemühen geht in Richtung einer konkreten Architektur, die «wie ein Blatt oder Stein» ist, nicht mehr Diskurs über die Wirklichkeit, sondern echte Transformation des Wirklichen vermittels einer abstrahierenden Praxis. Die jüngsten Entwürfe stellen auf diesem Weg des fortwährenden konzeptionellen Ringens um Konkretheit einen entscheidenden Schritt vorwärts dar. An Schule und Freizeitzentrum von Grand-Saconnex (13, 14) (zusammen in einem Gebäude untergebracht) zeigt sich, wie sich die «Ganzheit» verfestigt hat. Der vollständig mit ungleich breiten Quarzitplatten verkleidete Bau (die als Boden in die Holzschalung gelegt wurden und sich so mit dem darüber gegossenen Beton verbanden) erscheint als eine dunkle Masse. Ein großer Unterzug aus vorgespanntem Beton, eine Art T-Träger, dessen horizontale Flansche mit rechteckigen Lichtöffnungen durchbrochen sind, hält alle Räume, inklusive den als Empfang fungierenden Freiluftbereich, zusammen. Er gibt dem Projekt seinen dynamischen Zug. Im Außenbereich verleiht er der Zugangsterrasse einen Rahmen zum Himmel und zur tiefergelegenen Landschaft und macht sie zu einem Schwellenraum. Im Innenraum wird er, den jeweiligen Stand der Sonne durch ihren Schattenwurf anzeigend, zu einer Art Lichtmaschine. Auf den ebenmäßigen Beton- und Holzoberflächen können die Schatten klar hervortreten. Der Raum erhält auf diese Weise eine Tönung der Tageszeit. Die nach vorne ausgerichteten Klassenräume blicken mit großen Fenstern auf benachbart stehende Bäume. Die an die Rückseite gesetzten Räume weisen auf die Terrasse, von der aus eine weit sich erstreckende, halb natürliche, halb künstliche Landschaft zu sehen ist. In ihr findet das Gebäude seinen Sinn. Es ähnelt ein wenig einem Stein. Der Quarzit an den Fassaden trägt zur abstrakten Robustheit des Gesamten bei. «Sich eines Materials bedienen, das der Idee – nicht der Schule – des Unterrichtens so deutlich Rechnung trägt (Schiefer gestattet Kreidebemalung und damit Schrift), heißt fordern, daß Nutzung und Technik hier eine Einheit bilden, die auf dem Elementaren beruht – archaisch vielleicht – und die durch Gewicht, Rauheit, Nicht-Farbe zu einem nicht architektonischen Element geworden ist. Es gibt da nichts als Wände und Wandtafeln… Was den zwischen den Quarzitplatten in den Fugen sichtbaren Beton betrifft, so hinterläßt er die Spuren seiner Herstellung, seiner Robustheit und seiner Bestimmung, die wie auf sich selbst verweisen»[27]. Dieser düstere und stille Felsen ruht inmitten des Raums. Er, ein raffinierter Monolith, verströmt seine Ruhe weit über das Standortterrain hinaus in die Landschaft.

Ebenso wie die Schule von Grand-Saconnex verhält sich der Erweiterungsbau für das Gymnasium von Chamblandes (15, 16) [1992–96] zur umliegenden Landschaft[28]. Am Ufer des Genfer Sees errichtet, ergänzt das Gebäude zwei bereits früher entstandene Bauten, zu denen es sich in vertiefter Lage befindet. Als eleganter Riegel ist es eingeschoben zwischen eine Terrasse und Bäume. In seiner

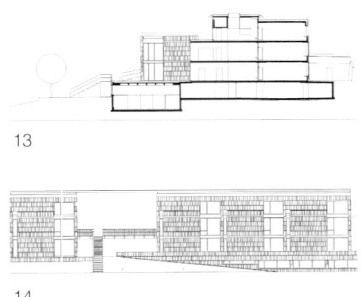

13

14

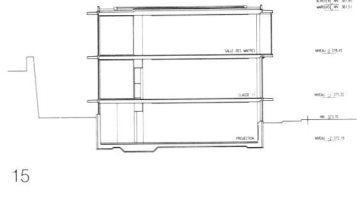

15

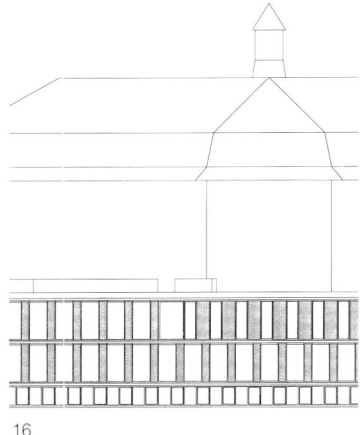

16

them, sculpture tends to 'unite itself with the milieu in which it exists', and this union with space 'must be realized not only with the portion of space in which the sculpture is located, but also with the totality of unlimited space'[29]. At Chamblandes, the architecture absorbs the surrounding milieu. It transforms a planar vision of the landscape into a global apprehension of the empty volume adhering to it. The oblong rectangle of the roof terrace defines an active horizontal plane, weighted to the ground by the 'feeling of a base' procured by the access from the north side to the building's roof. This plane is solid. The landscape can bounce back on it[30]. On the south side, seen from the garden, the building seems poised. Its facade develops a regular rhythm, based on the subtlety of its proportions and the relationships between the materials: the grey concrete of the structural frame, the aluminum frames, the translucent resin of the opening windows. This composite, which resembles glass tiles, forms a dialogue with the real glass and the lake shore. It coagulates the light and the water in its greenish texture structured with black threads. Adapted to its site, the architecture is discreet, almost invisible. Like the restoration projects, but following an inverse process[31], it merges into a reality which it transforms.

The house at Cugy (1994–96) confirms this imperceptible character[32]. A half-submerged barge, it eludes all sterile rules and, like a precious mineral, buries in the ground treasures of light and space 'IRIS Yellow water iris...'. Half embedded in the ground it is, through the framing of its volumes, closer to the sky. It is sailing somewhere out of the water, between being there and non-being, astonished at its own presence in this place. 'IRIS. Blue eyes, black eyes, green eyes are those whose iris is blue, is black, is green'[33].

Joseph Abram, January 1996

1- *René Char, 'La Bibliothèque est en feu', in Les Matinaux, suivi de La Parole en archipel, NRF, Poésie/Gallimard, Paris 1987, pp. 145–46 (first edition 1962).*

2- *Inès Lamunière, 'Matière et Fabrique, leçon inaugurale', in: DA-Informations, no. 165, EPFL, Département d'Architecture, 1995, pp. 4–20.*

3- *René Char, 'La Bibliothèque est en feu', op. cit., p. 146.*

4- *IL & PD followed the teaching of Kenneth Frampton at the Ecole Polytechnique Fédérale of Lausanne. From 1985 to 1988 she was assistant to Werner Oechslin at the Ecole Polytechnique Fédérale of Zurich. She now teaches at the EPFL. From 1984 to 1990 Patrick Devanthéry was assistant to Bruno Reichlin at the Ecole d'Architecture de Genève.*

5- *Cf. Patrick Devanthéry and Inès Lamunière, 'D'une géométrie baroque: licence ou règle?', in: DA-Informations, no. 66, EPFL, Département d'Architecture, Feb. 1984, pp. 3–22.*

6- *On these projects cf. Positions. Projets et réalisations: Patrick Devanthéry Inès Lamunière. Patrick Mestelan et Bernard Gachet, Thomas Boga, Zurich 1988.*

Erscheinung vereint es Elemente sehr unterschiedlicher Dimension und Wesensart. Von Norden wirkt es im Hintergrund des Hofs wie ein Sockel (oder vielmehr wie die Kante eines Sockels, der sich zum Vorteil des bereits Bestehenden nunmehr erst abzeichnet). Seine Niedrigkeit und die Verkleidung aus grau-gelbem Saint-Triphon-Stein (aus dem die alten Gebäude erbaut sind) lassen es zu dieser Seite hin als klar dem Unterbau zugehörig erscheinen. Im Süden ist sein Effekt ein dreifacher: Der Portalvorbau gibt Durchsicht auf Bäume und Wasser und rahmt diesen Ausblick als tiefengestuftes Landschaftsgemälde. Die Südfassade, an der wandhohe Glaspanele mit ebenso hohen engeren Öffnungen abwechseln, inszeniert die Seesicht mehr als ein Kontinuum. Das als Aussichtsplattform dienende Dach schließlich verwandelt das pittoreske Panorama in ein sehr zeitgenössisches, denn hinter der horizontalen Terrassenebene richten sich Garten, See und umliegende Berge zu einem steilflächigen Gesamtbild auf, das sich mit einem Blick fassen läßt. Das Wirkungsfeld des Gebäudes reicht so bis in weite Ferne, womit für die Architektur der räumliche Traum mancher Künstler der 30er Jahre erfüllt wäre. In einem Text von Wladyslaw Strzeminski und Katarzyna Kobro über die «Komposition des Raums», der vieles an Späterem bereits vorwegnimmt, heißt es, die Skulptur kenne a priori keine Grenzen, diese seien ihr nachträglich gesetzt. Die Skulptur strebe danach, «sich mit dem Milieu, in dem sie existiert, zu vereinen» und eine solche Union «sollte stattfinden nicht nur mit einem Teil des Raums, in dem sie sich unmittelbar befindet, sondern weiterreichen in die Totalität des unbegrenzten Raums...»[29]. In Chamblandes nimmt die Architektur das sie umgebende Milieu in sich auf. Sie transformiert die Wahrnehmung der Landschaft, die, vorher flächenhaft erscheinend, nunmehr Körperlichkeit erhält, sich wie im Winkel um ein ihr anhaftendes Leervolumen schmiegt. Das langgestreckte Rechteck der Dachterrasse definiert eine klare horizontale Ebene, die dadurch dem Erdboden verbunden bleibt, daß man von der Nordseite des Gebäudes Zugang zu ihr findet, und wo jener «Eindruck von Sockelhaftigkeit» sich vermittelt. Die Ebene ist eine solide. Die Landschaft kann sich an ihr emporrichten[30]. Die Südseite des Gebäudes, die man vom Garten aus sieht, wirkt zurückgenommen ruhig. Die Fassade weist hier einen gleichmäßigen Rhythmus auf, der auf Materialspiel und subtilen Maßsetzungen beruht: grauer Beton der horizontalen Bauteile, Aluminium der Fenstereinfassungen, transluzider Kunstharz der schmalen Fenster. Letzterer Kompositwerkstoff, in seiner Wirkung ähnlich dem Milchglas, tritt in einen Dialog mit dem echten Glas und gleichzeitig mit dem See. Licht und Wasser gerinnen in dem mit schwarzen Karbonfäden armierten, grünlichem Kunstharz zu einer Masse. Sich der Umgebung anpassend, ist die Architektur insgesamt diskret, ja fast unsichtbar. Wie die Restaurierungen, obgleich aus umgekehrtem Prozeß hervorgegangen[31], gründet sie auf dem Wirklichen und transformiert es zugleich.

Das Wohnhaus in Cugy (1994–96) gibt sich ähnlich zurückgenommen[32]. Wirkend wie ein

7- Martin Steinmann and Philippe Gueissaz, 'Le temps des signes, bâtiment de service à Villars-Ste-Croix VD, réalisé par Patrick Devanthéry et Inès Lamunière, in: Faces no. 16, Summer 1990, pp. 22–28. One senses here that the affection that Patrick Devanthéry and Inès Lamunière have for Robert Venturi and Denise Scott Brown, has left them an infinite sensitivity towards ordinary reality.

8- Bruno Reichlin, 'La forme du mouvement, architectes Patrick Devanthéry Inès Lamunière', in: Faces no. 32, Summer 1994, pp. 30–35.

9- It is interesting to compare this building to that on the Burgfelder Platz, by Diener and Diener (1982–85), in Basel, which is also conceived as an assemblage. This comparison shows two similar approaches of complexity.

10- On this building cf. Patrick Devanthéry and Inès Lamunière, 'Tout existe et rien n'est équivalent' in: Positions. Projets et réalisations, op. cit., pp. 34–38. Also cf. 'Logements étudiants, Genève', AMC no. 58, Feb. 1995, pp. 18–19.

11- Cf. Patrick Devanthéry and Inès Lamunière, 'Haute pression' in: Un centre d'arts plastiques contemporain à Lausanne. Cinq architectes, cinq projets, Musée des Arts Décoratifs de Lausanne, 1992, pp. 30–36.

12- André Ducret and Catherine Dumont d'Ayot, 'Visible/invisible, commande d'avant-projet pour un centre d'arts plastiques contemporain à Lausanne', in: Faces no. 26, Winter 1992, pp. 20–25.

13- Inès Lamunière, 'Matière et Fabrique', op. cit.

14- Alberto Grimoldi, 'Les bains de Bellerive-Plage, la matière travaillée ou le temps retrouvé', in: Faces no. 29, Autumn 1993, pp. 43–48.

15- Inès Lamunière, 'Matière et Fabrique', op. cit.

16- 'This strict and precise awareness of their own tasks protects them from the sterile ambition of leaving their own striking mark on an existing building at any price. The line of technical competence allowing the preservation is enough'. Cf. Alberto Grimoldi, 'Les bains de Bellerive-Plage', op. cit.

17- Cf. 'Patrick Devanthéry et Inès Lamunière: spazio musicale a Ginevra, 1990', Revista Technica no. 3, 1991, pp. 48–49.

18- Patrick Devanthéry and Inès Lamunière, 'Maison familiale, Cully, VD'. Architecture suisse, no. 80, December 1987, pp. 7–10.

19- Cf. Robert Ruata, 'Bibliothèque, architectes: Inès Lamunière et Patrick Devanthéry', in: Faces, no. 23, Spring 1992, pp. 9–10.

20- Cf. Patrick Devanthéry and Inès Lamunière, 'Extension suisse, maison B., Carouge-Genève', AMC no. 32-33, June–July 1992, p. 78.

21- Hans Frei, 'Annexe à Carouge, 1990', in: Faces no. 23, Spring 1992, pp. 20–21.

22- Max Bill, Robert Maillart, Zurich 1949, p. 29. Quoted by Inès Lamunière in 'Matière et Fabrique', op. cit.

23- 'Life is the goal of art. Art can misunderstand its own means and merely reflect life instead of creating it, thus its means are illusionist, descriptive, academic…'. Hans Arp, letter to Brzekowski, 1929, published in Abstraction Création, 1931–1939, Musée d'Art Moderne de la Ville de Paris, 1978, p. 59.

24- The exhibition at Lucerne brought together very different artists: Arp, Braque, Calder, Chirico, Derain, Ernst, Fernandez, Giacometti, Gonzales, Gris, Hélion, Kandinsky, Klee, Léger, Mondrian, Nicholson, Paalen, Picasso and Sophie Täuber.

25- Jean Hélion, quoted by Gladys-C. Fabre in her essay in the catalogue Abstraction Création, 1931–39, Musée d'Art Moderne de la Ville de Paris, 1978, pp. 26–27.

schon halb versunkener, gekenterter Kahn, entzieht es sich jedem sterilen Reglement und trägt wie ein kostbares Erz die Schätze von Licht und Raum in die Erde hinein. «Iris... gelbe Wasserschwertlilie...» Es ist zwar zur Hälfte in die Erde eingegraben, doch lassen die Einschnitte in das Raumvolumen das Haus näher dem Himmel erscheinen. Es bewegt sich irgendwo jenseits der Meere, zwischen Dasein und Nicht-Sein, erstaunt über seine eigene Präsenz an diesem Ort. «Iris. Blaue Augen, schwarze Augen, grüne Augen sind solche, deren Regenbogenhaut (Iris) blau ist, schwarz ist, grün ist»[33].

Joseph Abram, Januar 1996

1- *René Char, «La Bibliothèque est en feu»/«Die Bibliothek steht in Flammen», in: ders., Poésie (Teils. frz. u. dt.), Frankfurt a.M. 1959, S. 351.*

2- *Inès Lamunière, «Matière et Fabrique, leçon inaugurale», in: DA-Informations Nr.165, EPFL, Département d'Architecture, 1995, S. 4–20.*

3- *René Char, «La Bibliothèque est en feu»/«Die Bibliothek steht in Flammen», in: ders., Poésie, a.a.O., S. 353.*

4- *IL & PD hörte an der Eidgenössischen Technischen Hochschule (EPFL) von Lausanne die Vorlesungen Kenneth Framptons. 1985–88 war sie Assistentin Werner Oechslins an der ETH Zürich. Heute lehrt sie an der EPFL. Patrick Devanthéry war 1984–90 Assistent von Bruno Reichlin an der Architekturhochschule Genf.*

5- *Vgl. Patrick Devanthéry und Inès Lamunière, «D'une géométrie baroque: licence ou règle?», in: Da-Informations Nr. 66, EPFL, Département d'Architecture, Februar 1984, S. 3–22.*

6- *Vgl. zu diesen Projekten: «Positions, Projets et réalisations: Patrick Devanthéry et Inès Lamunière. Patrick Mestelan et Bernard Gachet», Thomas Boga, Zürich, 1988.*

7- *Martin Steinmann und Philippe Gueissaz, «Le temps des signes, bâtiment de service à Villars-Ste-Croix VD, réalisé par Patrick Devanthéry et Inès Lamunière», in: Faces Nr. 16, Sommer 1990, S. 22–28. In diesem Artikel deutet sich an, daß vielleicht die Einflüsse Robert Venturis und Denise Scott Browns auf Patrick Devanthéry und Inès Lamunière dazu beitrugen, daß diese den Wert der alltäglichen Wirklichkeit so hoch zu schätzen lernten.*

8- *Bruno Reichlin, «La forme du mouvement, architectes: Patrick Devanthéry et Inès Lamunière», in: Faces Nr. 32, Sommer 1994, S. 30–35.*

9- *Es ist interessant, dieses Gebäude mit dem vom Burgfelder Platz in Basel (Diener und Diener 1982–85) zu vergleichen, dem ebenso der Ansatz eines Versammelns vieler Einzelelemente zugrunde liegt. Der Umgang mit Komplexität ist hier ein sehr ähnlicher.*

10- *Vgl. zu diesem Gebäude: Patrick Devanthéry und Inès Lamunière, «Tout existe et rien n'est équivalent», in: Positions, Projets et réalisations, a.a.O., S. 34–38. Vgl. auch «Logements étudiants, Genève», in: AMC Nr. 58, Februar 1995, S. 18–19.*

11- *Vgl. Patrick Devanthéry und Inès Lamunière, «Haute pression», in: Un centre d'arts plastiques contemporain à Lausanne. Cinq architectes, cinq projets, Musée des Arts Décoratifs de Lausanne, 1992, S. 30–36.*

12- *André Ducret und Catherine Dumont d'Ayot, «Visible/invisible, commande d'avant-projet pour un centre d'arts plastiques contemporain à Lausanne», in: Faces Nr. 26, Winter 1992, S. 20–25.*

26- M. Evans, 'Hélion to-day', in: Axis, no. 4, 1935, pp. 4–9, quoted by Gladys-C. Fabre, op. cit.

27- Inès Lamunière in 'Matière et Fabrique', op. cit., p. 17.

28- Patrick Devanthéry and Inès Lamunière, 'Vers une douce rhétorique?' in: Archithese no. 4, 1993, pp. 24–27.

29- W. Streminski and K. Kobro, 'La composition de l'espace. Les calculs du rhythme spatio-temporel', in: W. Streminski and K. Kobro, L'Espace Uniste, écrits du constructivisme polonais. L'Age d'Homme, Lausanne 1977, p. 87.

30- A similar poetry is found in the work of Livio Vacchini. From his first projects onwards (the metal grammar school) Vacchini used the ground as a platform to propel the project towards the landscape. The architecture captures the near and distant space. Horizontal planes play an active role: the terrace at Montagnola (we forget we are on the roof of a school) and the mighty overhanging roof of the Lido at Ascona are at the scale of the surrounding mountains.

31- Like the restoration project (which closes upon an existing reality) the project for a new building (after having opened onto an infinity of possibilities) closes upon a future reality. The arbitrariness of this closing induces an exigence: the project must find in the real an infinite number of reasons for its uniqueness.

32- The project called for an extension to a family house, but which constitutes in reality, an independent house sharing an existing wall. This 'furtive' house, almost invisible in this place, might symbolically have no address.

33- René Char, 'Sur le franc-bord', in: Les Matinaux, suivi de La parole en archipel, NRF, Poésie/Gallimard, Paris 1987, p. 100. 'I. IRIS. 1. Name of a divinity of Greek mythology who was the messenger of the gods… 2. Woman's name used by poets to designate a beloved woman or even some lady whose name they wish to conceal. 3. Small planet. / II. Generic name of a butterfly, the grey nymphalid, called the iridescent emperor… / III. IRIS. Blue eyes, black eyes, green eyes… / IV. IRIS. Genus of plant. Yellow water iris…' (René Char).

13- Inès Lamunière, «Matière et Fabrique», a.a.O.

14- Alberto Grimoldi, «Les bains de Bellerive-Plage, la matière travaillée ou le temps retrouvé», in: Faces Nr. 29, Herbst 1993, S. 43–48.

15- Inès Lamunière, «Matière et Fabrique», a.a.O.

16- «Ein solch strenges und präzises Gespür für die eigenen Aufgaben schützt vor der unfruchtbaren Ambition, dem Bestehenden um jeden Preis einen ins Auge springenden Stempel aufzudrücken. Eine Linie gezeichnet von technischer Kompetenz, die den Erhalt gestattet, genügt.» Vgl. Alberto Grimoldi, «Les bains de Bellerive-Plage ...», a.a.O.

17- Vgl. «Patrick Devanthéry et Inès Lamunière: spazio musicale à Ginevra, 1990», in: Revista Technica Nr. 3, 1991, S. 48–49.

18- Patrick Devanthéry und Inès Lamunière, «Maison Familiale, Cully, VD», in: Architecture suisse Nr. 80, Dezember 1987, S. 7–10.

19- Vgl. Robert Ruata, «Bibliothèque, architectes: Inès Lamunière et Patrick Devanthéry», in: Faces Nr. 23, Frühling 1992, S. 9–10.

20- Vgl. Patrick Devanthéry und Inès Lamunière, «Extension suisse, maison B., Carouge-Genève», in: AMC Nr. 32-33, Juni–Juli 1992, S.78.

21- Hans Frei, «Annexe à Carouge, 1990», in: Faces Nr. 23, Frühling 1992, S. 20–21.

22- Max Bill, Robert Maillart, Zürich 1949, S. 29, zitiert von Inès Lamunière in «Matière et Fabrique», a.a.O.

23- «Auf Leben zielt die Kunst hin. Die Kunst kann aber ihre Mittel verkennen und das Leben nur betrachten anstatt es zu schöpfen, dann verfährt sie illusionistisch, beschreibend, akademisch...», Hans Arp in einem Brief an Brzekowski von 1929, publiziert in: Abstraction Création, 1931–1939, Musée d'Art Moderne de la Ville de Paris, 1978, S. 59.

24- In der Ausstellung von Luzern waren sehr unterschiedliche Künstler versammelt: Arp, Braque, Calder, Chirico, Derain, Ernst, Fernandez, Giacometti, Gonzales, Gris, Hélion, Kandinsky, Klee, Léger, Mondrian, Nicholsohn, Paalen, Picasso und Sophie Täuber.

25- Jean Hélion zitiert nach dem Essay von Gladys-C. Fabre im Katalog Abstraction Création, 1931–1939", Musée d'Art Moderne de la Ville de Paris, 1978, S. 59.

26- M. Evans, «Hélion today», in: Axis Nr. 4, 1935, S. 4–9.

27- Inès Lamunière, «Matière et Fabrique», a.a.O., S. 17.

28- Patrick Devanthéry und Inès Lamunière, «Vers une douce rhétorique?», in: Archithese Nr. 4, 1993, S. 24–27.

29- W. Streminski et K. Kobro, «La composition de l'espace. Les calculs du rythme spatio-temporel», in W. Streminski et K. Kobro, L'Espace Uniste, écrits du constructivisme polonais, L'Age d'Homme, Lausanne, 1977, p. 87.

30- Man findet eine ähnliche Form von Poesie bei Livio Vacchini. Schon in seinen ersten Entwürfen (z. B. beim «metallenen Gymnasium») nutzt Vacchini die Bodenebene als eine Plattform zum Sprung in die Landschaft. Die Architektur fängt den nahen und fernen Raum ein. Die horizontalen Flächen haben hieran aktiven Anteil: die Terrasse von Montagnola (man vergißt, daß man sich auf dem Dach einer Turnhalle befindet) und das mächtige Überhangdach am Lido von Ascona halten den umgebenden Bergen stand.

31- Wie der Restaurierungsentwurf eine existierende Wirklichkeit einschließt, bezieht sich das Projekt für ein neues Gebäude (nachdem es sich einem Unendlichen an Möglichkeiten geöffnet hat) auf eine kommende Wirklichkeit. Seine endgültige Gestalt verliert ihre Willkür, da hinter ihr eine Forderung steht: der Entwurf muß im Wirklichen unzählige Gründe für seine Einheit finden.

32- Es ging um die Erweiterung eines Einfamilienhauses; enstanden ist aber letztlich ein eigenständiger Hausteil. Es wäre diesem «verstohlenen», in der Gegend fast unsichtbaren Haus gewissermaßen angemessen, ohne Adresse zu bleiben.

33- René Char, «Sur le franc bord»/«Am Saum des Fusses», in: ders., Poésie, a.a.O., S. 331, «I. IRIS 1. Name einer Gottheit aus der griechischen Mythologie; sie war Botin der Götter [...] 2. Weiblicher Eigenname, dessen die Dichter sich bedienen, um eine geliebte Frau zu bezeichnen oder auch eine Dame, deren Name verschwiegen werden soll. 3. Kleiner Planet. / II. IRIS Gattungsname eines Schmetterlings, der graue Nymphalide, Schillerfalter genannt [...] / III. IRIS Blaue Augen, schwarze Augen, grüne Augen sind solche, deren Regenbogenhaut (Iris) blau ist, schwarz ist, grün ist. / IV. IRIS Pflanzengattung. Gelbe Wasserschwertlilie [...]»

AUSSTELLEN

«Four examples» vergegenwärtigt eine kleine Auswahl jener «Entwurfs-Gelegenheiten», die oft unter zufälligen Umständen entstehen und hier nun zur Ausstellung gelangen. Fast ein Paradox ist dieser Versuch, etwas in Anschauung zu bringen, das doch für uns vor allem Freude am Machen bedeutet und ein paar Bekenntnisse…

Von außen gibt es nichts zu sehen – es sei denn man sei neugierig und wißbegierig. Der Betrachter hier ist ein einsamer, dem die spezifisch-kultische Sichtweise des Kamera-Auges aufgezwungen wird. Schrittbewegungen, Entfernungen und Blickwinkel sind vorgegeben um einen so in ein Zwiegespräch mit drei kleinen Video-Monitoren eintauchen zu lassen, die für je einen der Bauten stehen. Sie nehmen einen sozusagen an der Hand und führen einen durch die Ausstellung, indem sie gleichzeitig jegliche Distanz aufheben.

Im Innern gilt es, die Gesamtheit zu erleben, eine Auswahl ist nicht erlaubt. Hier wirkt die Kraft der großen Leinwand. Die physische Präsenz verliert sich in der Räumlichkeit. Bewegungslos gibt man sich der verlockenden Wirkung von Gliederung, Lichtspiel und Material hin, die alle fast greifbar erscheinen.

Der Herstellungsprozeß dieser Architekturen wird in der Folge veranschaulicht durch die Präsenz der Ausführungspläne und Notizen, die ihrerseits beredte Spuren und Zeugen der Schwerkraft sind. Sie sind, vergleichbar mit den wundersamen Wurzeln des leichten Schilfrohrs, das sich übergangslos aus dem Gewässer gegen den Himmel reckt, die Erscheinung dessen, was man oftmals zu verbergen trachtet.

Der so angelegte Ausstellungsrundgang erscheint wie eine fortlaufende Metapher unserer Arbeit:

«Zum Sehen bringen», vielleicht, aber nur in präzisem Kontext. Die Architektur hat nichts anderes zu zeigen als das, was die Geschichte, oder besser deren Erfahrung, uns lehrt. In diesem Sinne geht es um ein Ausprobieren, Auswählen und Interpretieren von zwei, drei Gegebenheiten dieser Geschichte, von Geometrie, von Öffnungen und von Materialien. Dies mit dem Ziel, eine passende Antwort zu geben in bezug auf die Neuerfindung des Ortes und die Auslegung eines Bauprogrammes im weitesten Sinne des Wortes, das heißt, von der Nutzung bis zur Symbolik und von der Wirtschaftlichkeit bis zur gesellschaftlichen Bedeutung.

«Zum Sein bringen» das ist, wie auch immer, unsere gesellschaftliche Verantwortung. Durch die Rationalität seiner Anlage konkretisiert sich der Innenraum, die Art, wie die tragenden Strukturen gesetzt sind, bestimmt seine Nutzung, läßt ihn Körper annehmen und verleiht ihm Rhythmus. Der Lichteinfall wird gebändigt, frei flutend belassen oder gefiltert; ausschlaggebend dafür sind die Stimmungseffekte, die mit rohen, rauhen oder warmen Materialien erzeugt werden entsprechend dem angestrebten Grad von Häuslichkeit.

Das «Machen» läßt sich nicht zeigen. Pläne und Details als Gegenstände des architektonischen Alltags sagen jedoch das ihre zu jener «unmöglichen» Überbrückung der Trennung von Innen und Außen, die im Rundgang angelegt ist. Durch die Studien von Öffnungen in ihrer jeweiligen Besonderheit soll hier vor allem das Fenster zu Wort kommen, mit seinen klaren Nutzungsbestimmungen, den von ihm gezeichneten Proportionen und seiner atmenden Eleganz, das Fenster, dem die Rolle zufällt, Geschichten zu erzählen.

Patrick Devanthéry und
Inès Lamunière, März 1996

EXHIBITING

'Four examples' retraces a short series of those 'design occasions', often hazardous in their circumstances and, here, exhibited. Like a paradox, this is an offer to show what is primarily for us, perhaps, a pleasure to make and a few beliefs…

From the exterior, there is nothing to be seen, except being avid and curious. Here, it is a solitary voyeur constrained by the cult eye of the camera. The movement of footsteps, the distance and the glance are given in order to plunge face to face against three small colour screens which replace each one of the buildings. They take you by the hand and cancel the distance for your guided visit.

From the interior, everything is to be lived, the choice is not permitted. Here, it is through the virtuality of the large screen. The physical presence is drowned in the spatiality. Immobile but standing, the senses are invited to the spatial organisations, the light, the materials, almost to the sense of touch.

The fabrication of these architectures is represented by the knowledgeable explanation of working drawings, notes and witnesses of the contingencies of gravity. Like the amazing roots of a delicate reed emerging without transition from the pond to the sky, they are the manifestation of what one often wants to hide.

The path of the exhibition traced in this way appears like a sequential metamorphosis of our work:

'Giving to be seen', maybe, but only in a precise context. Architecture has nothing to show except what, with history, or better with its experience, it teaches us. So, testing, choosing, interpreting two or three things that we know about it, about geometry, about openings and materials in order to attempt an adequate answer to the invention of a place, to the interpretation of a program in the broad sense, from the functional to the symbolic, from economy to social uses.

'Giving to be', however, is our social responsibility. By the rationality of spatial organisations, interior space becomes concrete, by the invention of bearing structures, it allows use, takes shape and rhythm. The light here is mastered, accepted or filtered, dictated by the emotions of the created effects on rough materials, unrefined or warm depending on their degree of domesticity.

'Doing', is not to be shown. The everyday work of the plan and of details relate however this 'impossible' mediation of the cutting out of exterior-interior proposed by the exhibition's path. By the drawing of the opening, always specific, it is the window with the rigor of its uses, with the proportions it describes and with the elegance of its respirations that we would like to give the role to tell stories.

Patrick Devanthéry and
Inès Lamunière, March 1996

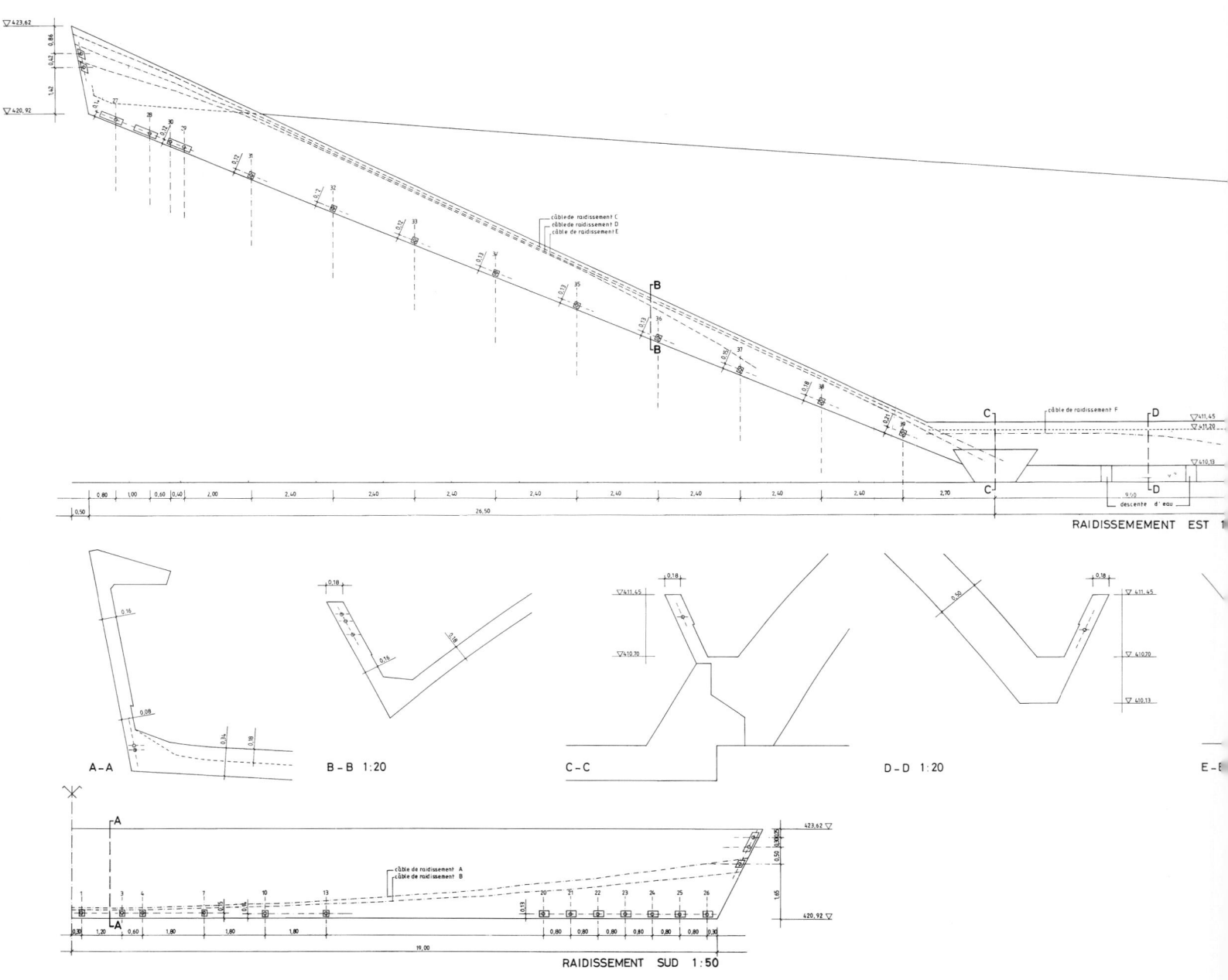

RAIDISSEMEMENT EST

RAIDISSEMENT SUD 1:50

LAUSANNE

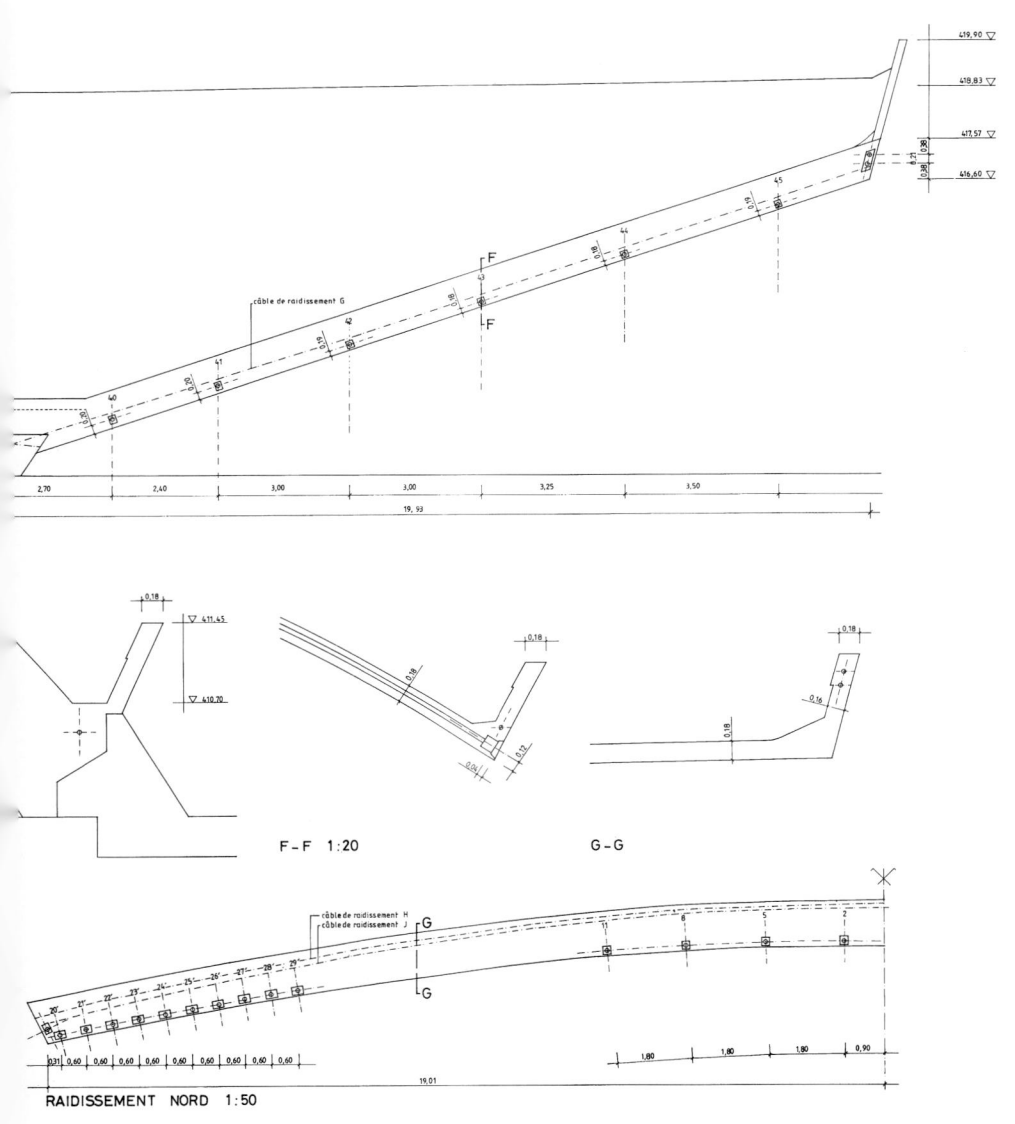

F-F 1:20   G-G

RAIDISSEMENT NORD 1:50

LAUSANNE

The assembly hall of the Ecole Polytechnique of Lausanne was built by the architect J. Tschumi and the engineer F. Panchaud in 1962. The building has taken on mythical significance in the history of reinforced concrete, using the most advanced technology of its time: a concrete thought to be waterproof, rough after removal of formworks, formed as a pre-stressed saddle. The concrete has suffered fatigue in the literal sense; the material has become deformed. Known in principle in the early 1960s, the phenomenon of creep in concrete was underestimated at that time; measurements of the deformation taken in 1994 confirmed the worst rumours: all the window supports were loaded and the shell was not self-supporting. Here, we restored the actual phenomenon of deformation, by cutting away the upper part of the vertical supports, allowing the shell to settle, and then repositioning it. Pressure gauges at the top of the window supports, acknowledge the impurity of a shape which is, nevertheless, so pure. This hybrid solution accomodates the overloading associated with the reconstruction of the outer surface of heavily carbonated and degraded concrete.

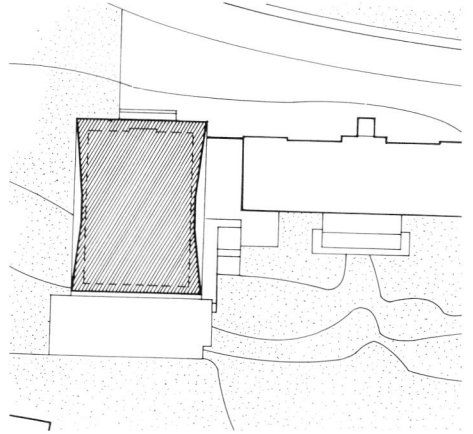

Die Aula der Eidgenössischen Polytechnischen Hochschule von Lausanne wurde 1962 vom Architekten J. Tschumi und dem Ingenieur F. Panchaud gebaut. Sie ist aufgrund der Kühnheit ihrer Technologie schon zu einem Mythos der Geschichte des Stahlbetonbaus geworden: ein wasserundurchlässig gedachter, schalungsrauher Beton, vorgespannt und in Sattelform gebracht. Der Beton ist im wahrsten Sinne des Wortes ermüdet; das Material hat sich deformiert. Das Phänomen des Kriechens war zwar in seinen Grundzügen zu Beginn der sechziger Jahre bereits bekannt, wurde jedoch allgemein unterschätzt; die 1994 bemessene Stärke der Verformungen hat die schlimmsten Prophezeiungen der damaligen Zeit bestätigt: alle Tragstreben der Glaswände sind überlastet und die Schale ist nicht selbsttragend. Wir haben in diesem Fall die Verformungserscheinung selbst in die Restaurierung miteinbezogen: die Senkrechtstreben der Glaswände wurden oben gekappt, das Betonsegel wurde abgesenkt und das Ganze erneut befestigt. Die Kontrollmanometer, die oben an den Streben angebracht wurden, sind ein augenzwinkernder Verweis auf die Unreinheit der scheinbar doch so reinen Form. Diese hybride Lösung läßt statisch auch die Zusatzlast zu, die sich aus der Ausbesserung und Wiederherstellung der stark karbonatisierten und angegriffenen Betonoberfläche ergibt.

PANNEAUX DE COFFRAGE DE L'INTRADOS
CÂBLE DE PRECONTRAINTE
ARMATURE
PROFONDEUR DE DEMOLITION
NU DU BANDEAU ACTUEL
LAMES DE COFFRAGES 60 MM / 2 M, RABOTEES
NOUVEAU MICROBETON
0 5 10 20 30 CM

TETE DE RECEPTION
PARCLOSE (U 40 26 3) DEPOSEE
TETE DE PILIER 300 92 6 DECOUPEE
CONTREFORT INT U 80 40 4 DECOUPE
PARCLOSE (L 25 92 3) DECOUPEE
PATTE D'ANGLE DE SUPPORT DE LA CARROSSERIE
PARCLOSE RECONSTITUEE
CARROSSERIE DE RHABILLAGE DU PILIER
PARCLOSE REPOSEE

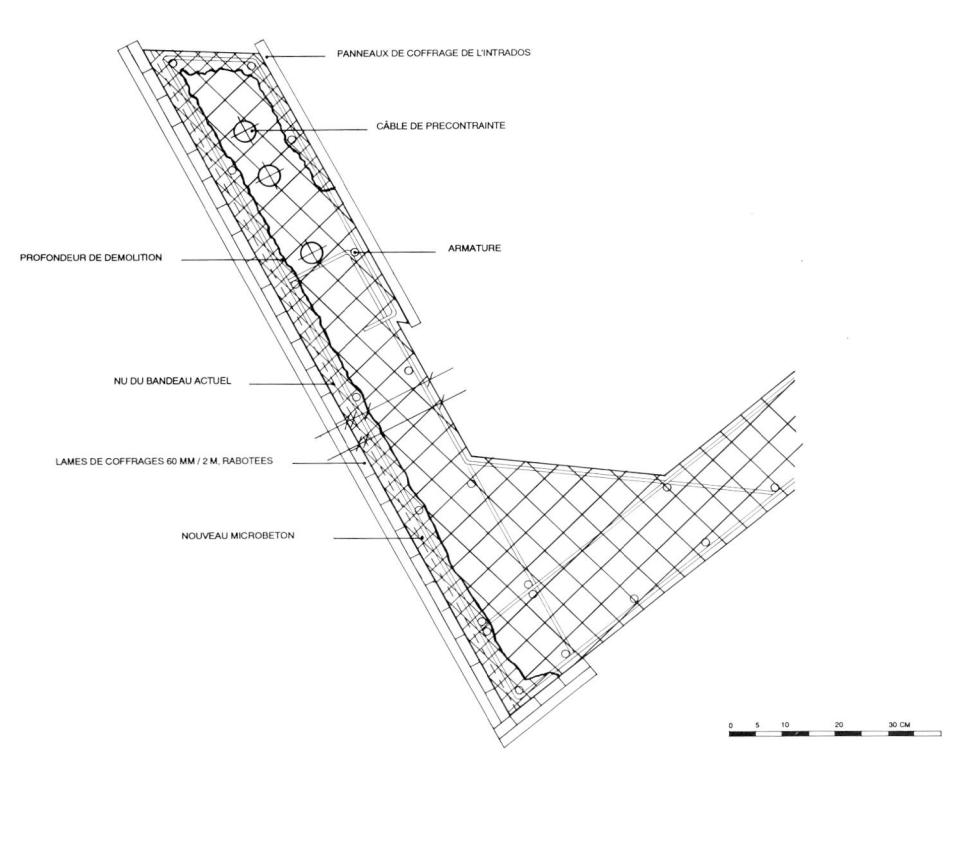

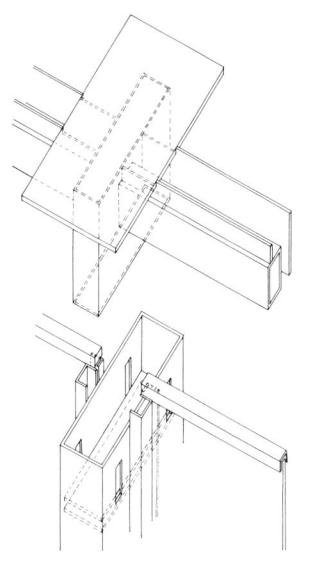

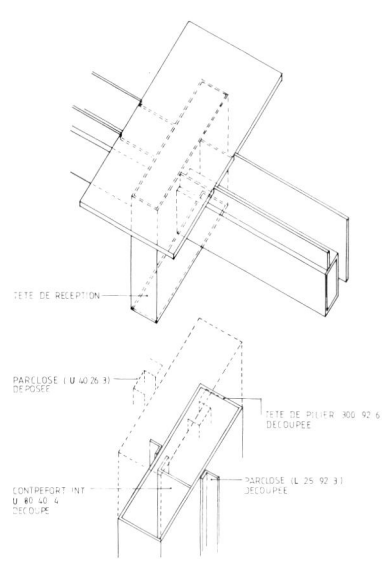

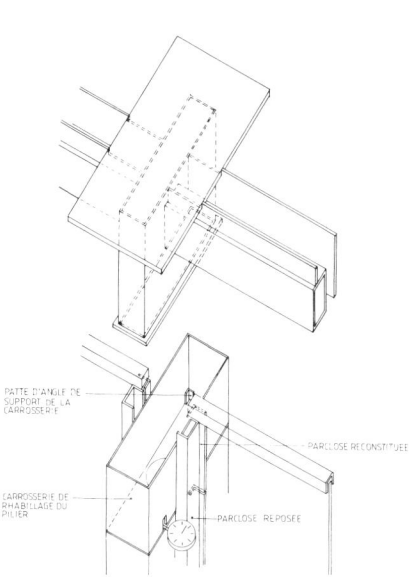

37

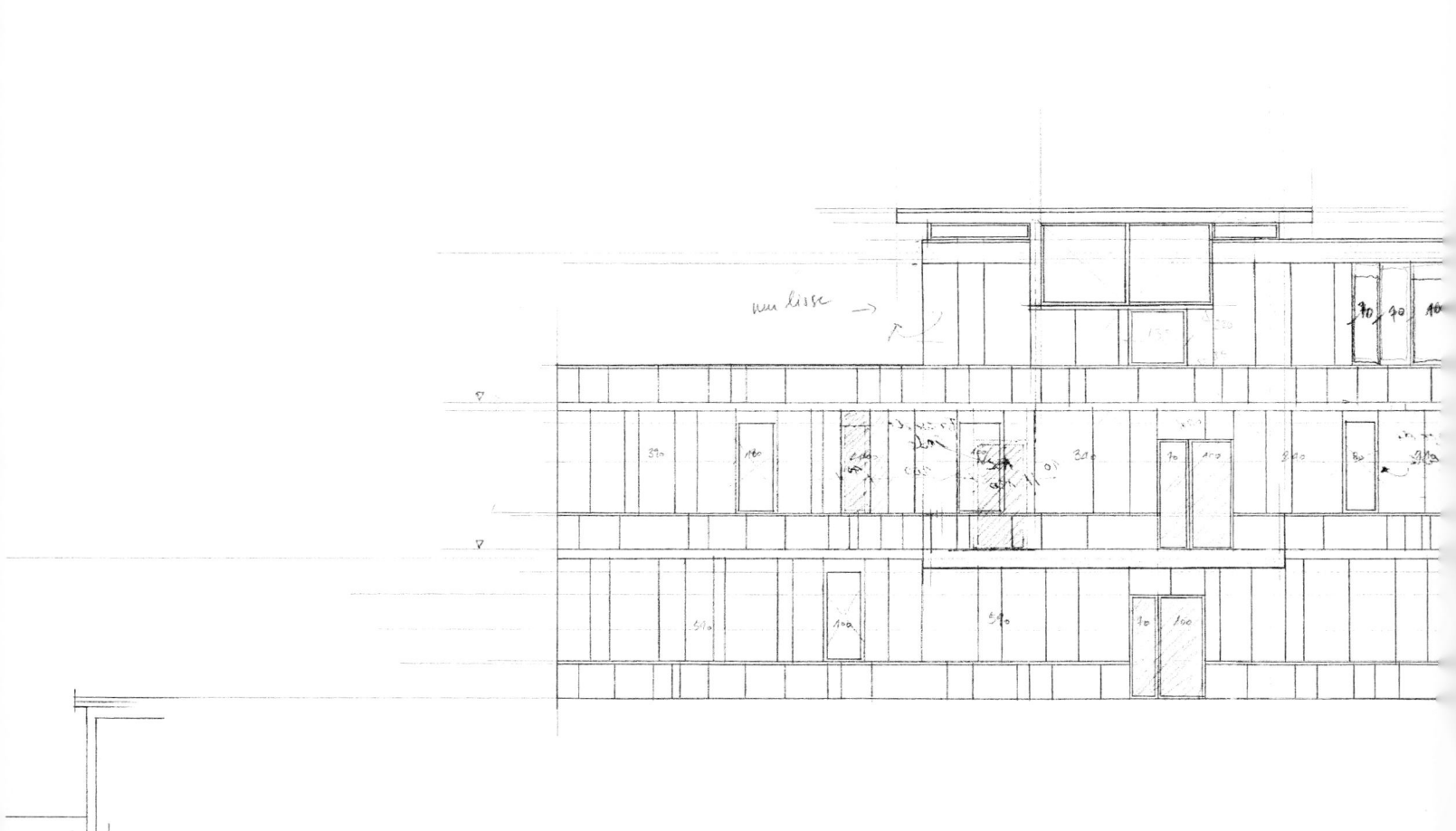

GRAND-SACONNEX

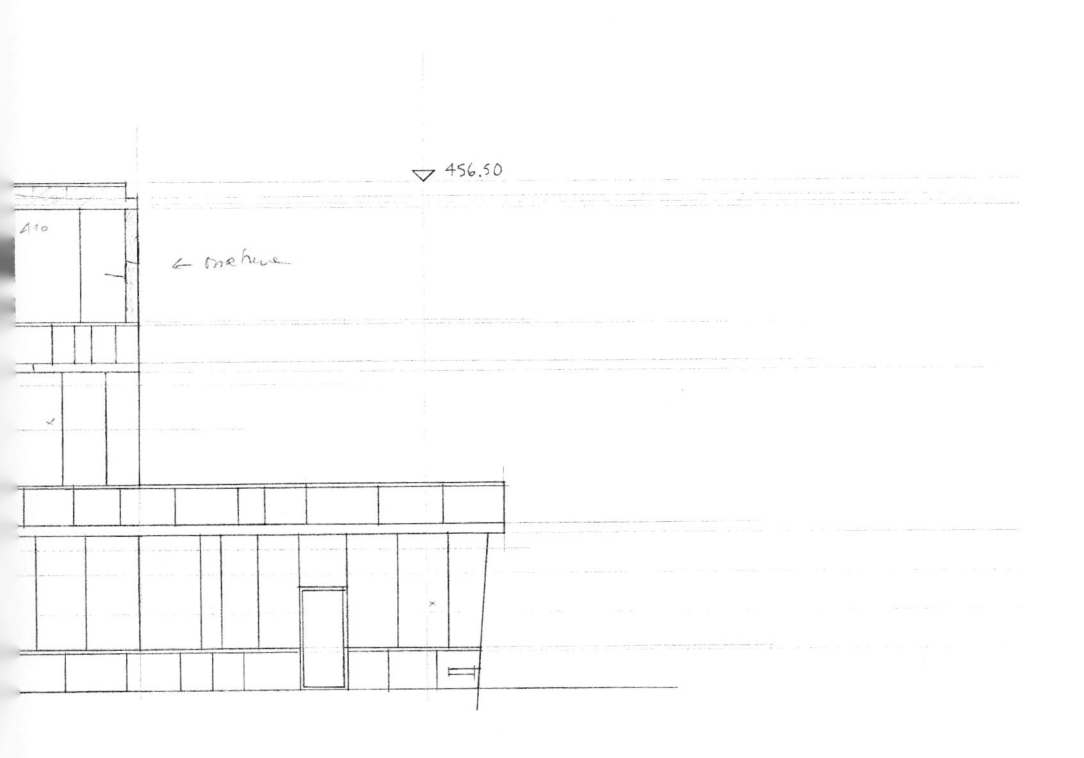

▽ 456.50

GRAND-SACONNEX

The primary school and leisure centre of Grand-Saconnex, close to Geneva, are united under a single perforated ridge beam of pre-stressed concrete. It covers a large open-air space which, facing the town hall, frames the landscape of the plateau and of the Jura, and recomposes the paths of the neighbourhoods below and above. On each side of this space, the large beam extends into the interior halls of the school and the centre, and distributes a dominant, referential lighting. The typical units formed by the classrooms are aligned, on the road side, with the future buildings along the road to Colovrex, while on the garden side, the layout 'takes its ease', with workshops for practical subjects set into the slope. All the facades are of split quartzite plaques placed randomly at the bottom of the formwork of the wall elements. This stone, related to the slate which allows chalk and writing, is also archaic through its weight, its roughness and its lack of colour: here we see only walls, boards, in which are inscribed holes, slits or glass panels.

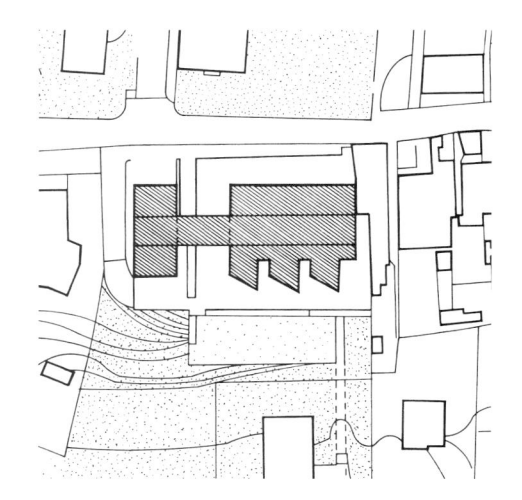

Grundschule und Freizeitzentrum von Grand-Saconnex, nahe bei Genf, sind unter einem gemeinsamen T-Träger aus vorgespanntem Beton zusammengefaßt, der mit rechteckigen Luken durchsetzt ist. Dieser überdeckt eine große, luftdurchflutete Eingangshalle, die – dem Rathaus gegenüberliegend – die Landschaft der Hochebene und des Juragebirges rahmt und die Quartiere oberhalb und unterhalb neu zueinander in Beziehung setzt. Diesseits und jenseits des «Luftraums» stößt der Träger in die innenliegenden Hallen der Schule, beziehungsweise des Zentrums vor und läßt dort auffällige Lichteffekte entstehen, die die Aufmerksamkeit auf sich ziehen. Die gleichförmigen Klassenzimmereinheiten reihen sich straßenseitig entlang der Baulinie für die geplante Route de Colovrex; Richtung Garten «lockert» sich die Anlage mit den Räumen für praktische Werkarbeit, die in den Hang geschmiegt sind, auf. Die Fassaden bestehen aus Quarzitplatten, die parallel zur geologischen Schichtung gespalten wurden; bei der Herstellung der Mauerelemente wurden die Quarzitplatten auf den Boden der Schalung gelegt, und die Fugen mit opus incertum ausgefüllt. Dieser Stein, verwandt mit dem Schiefer und eine Beschriftung mit Kreide erlaubt, hat durch sein Gewicht, seine Unebenheit und seine Nicht-Farbe einen archaischen Charakter: es gibt hier nur Wände, Wandtafeln und in Entsprechung dazu Löcher, Schlitze oder Glasflächen.

41

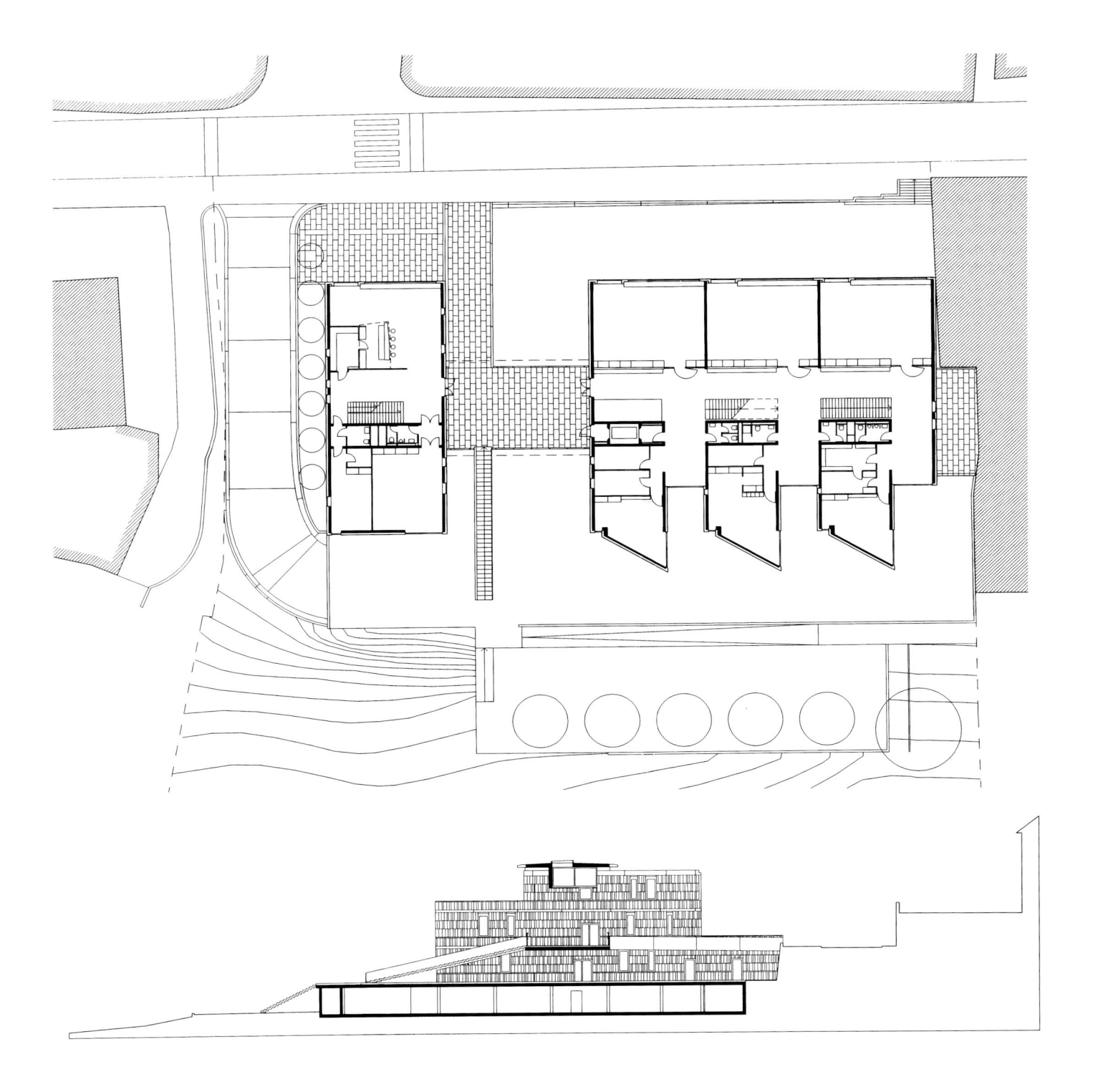

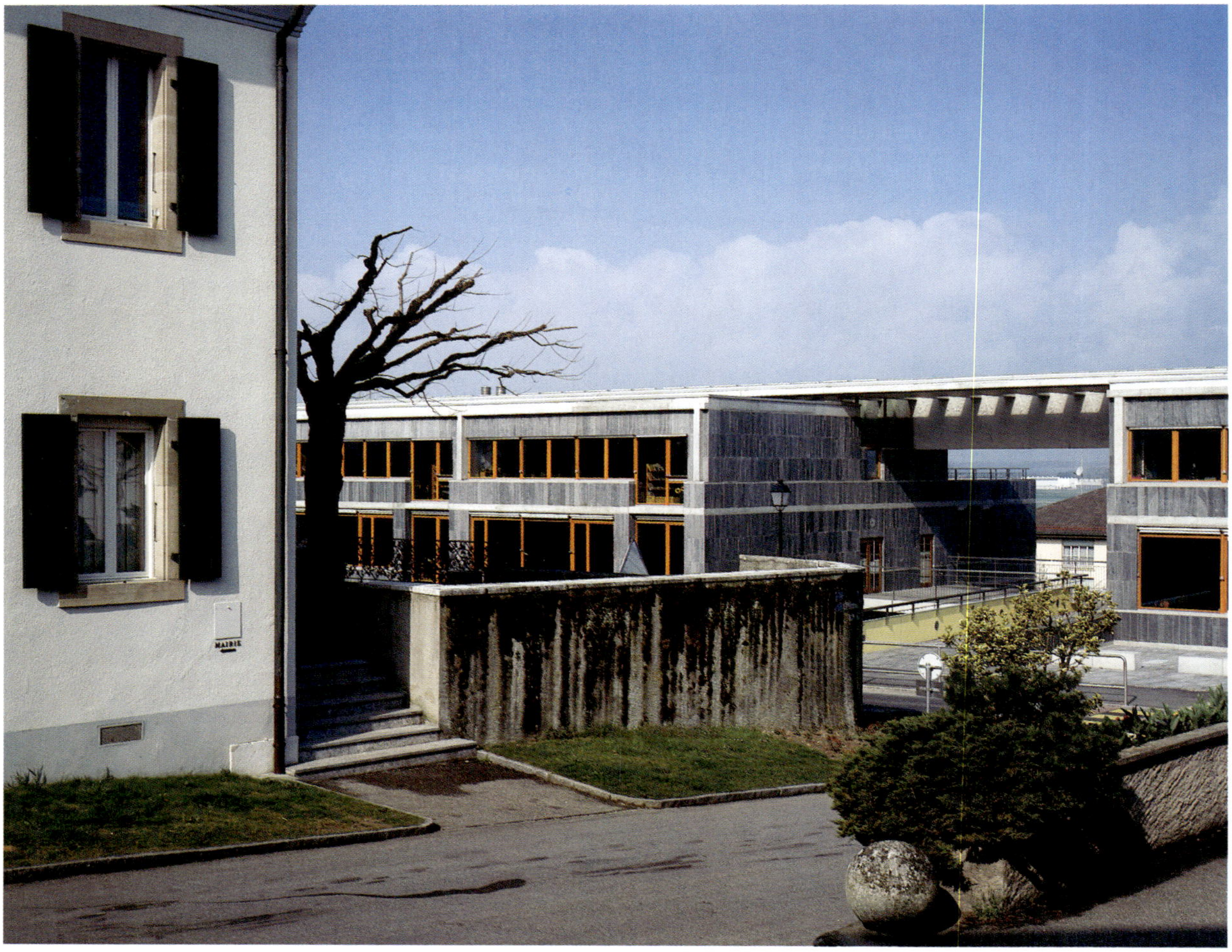

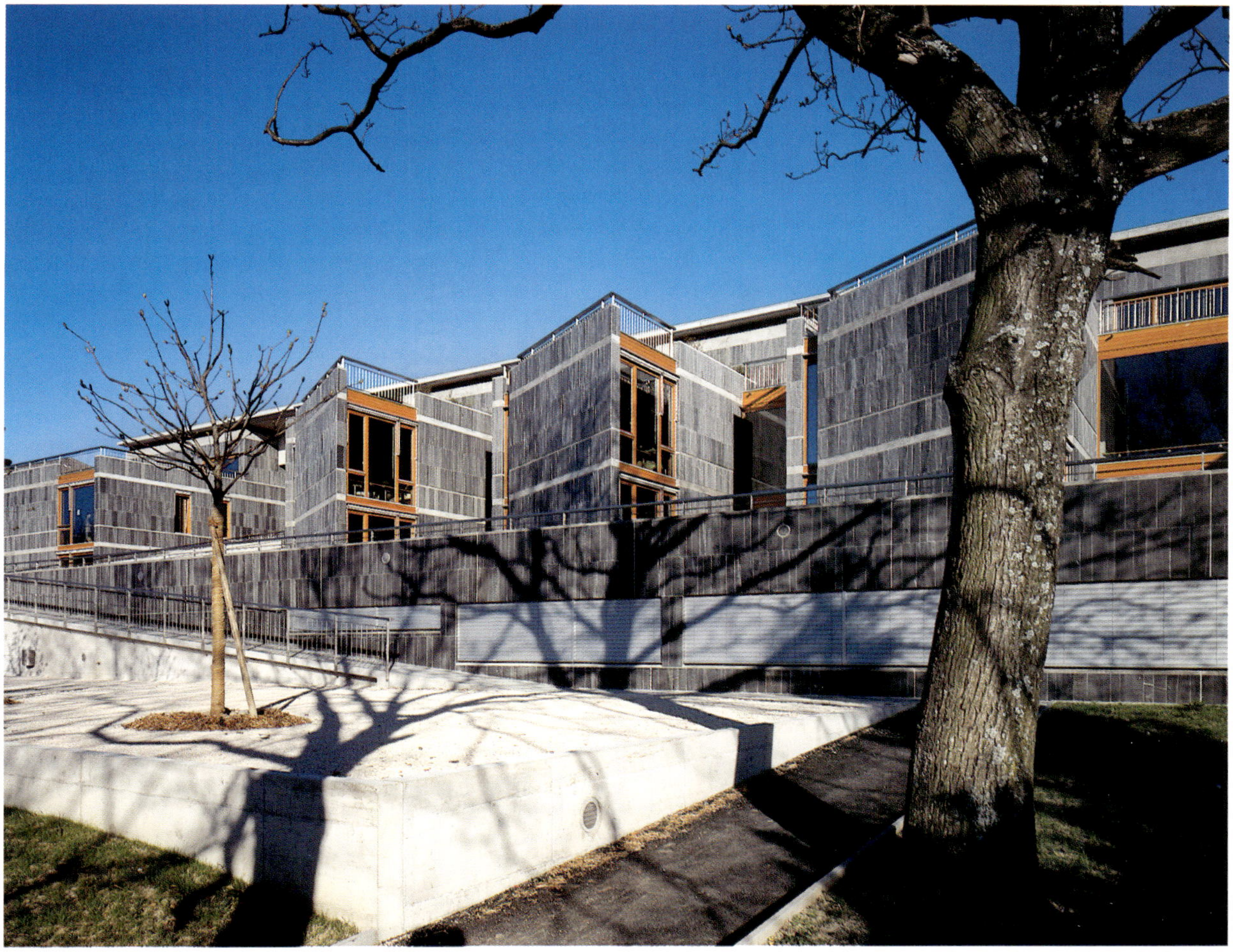

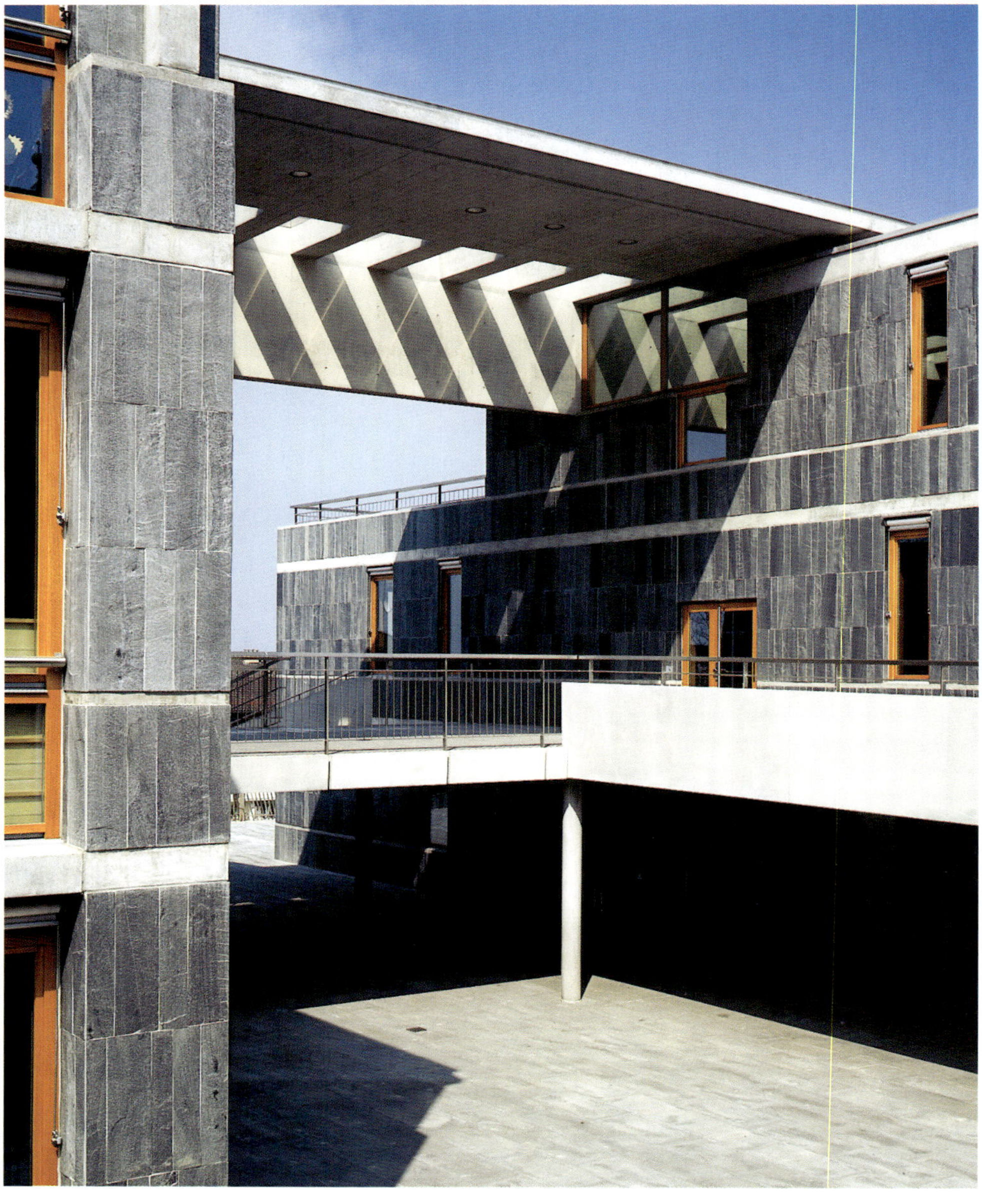

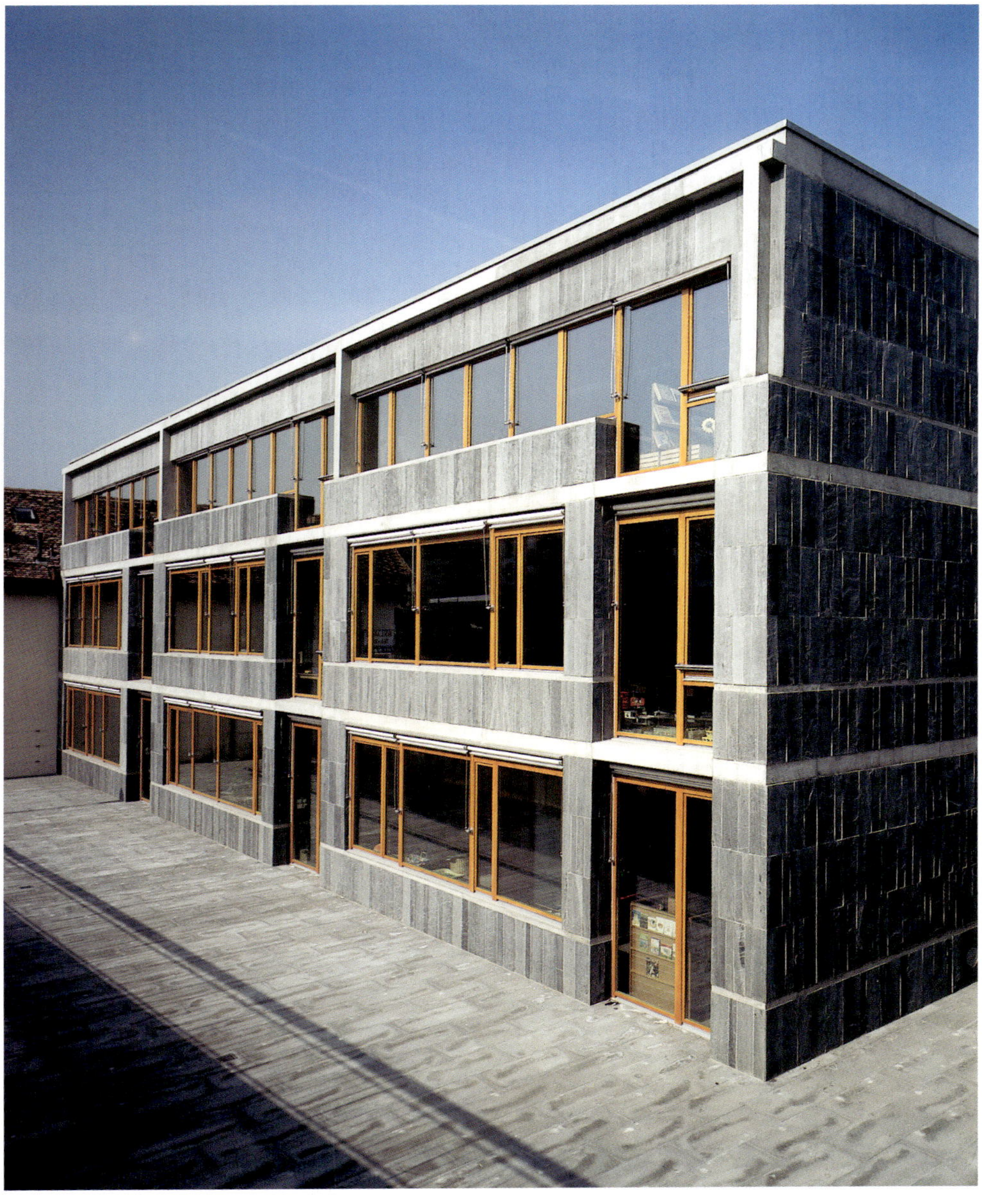

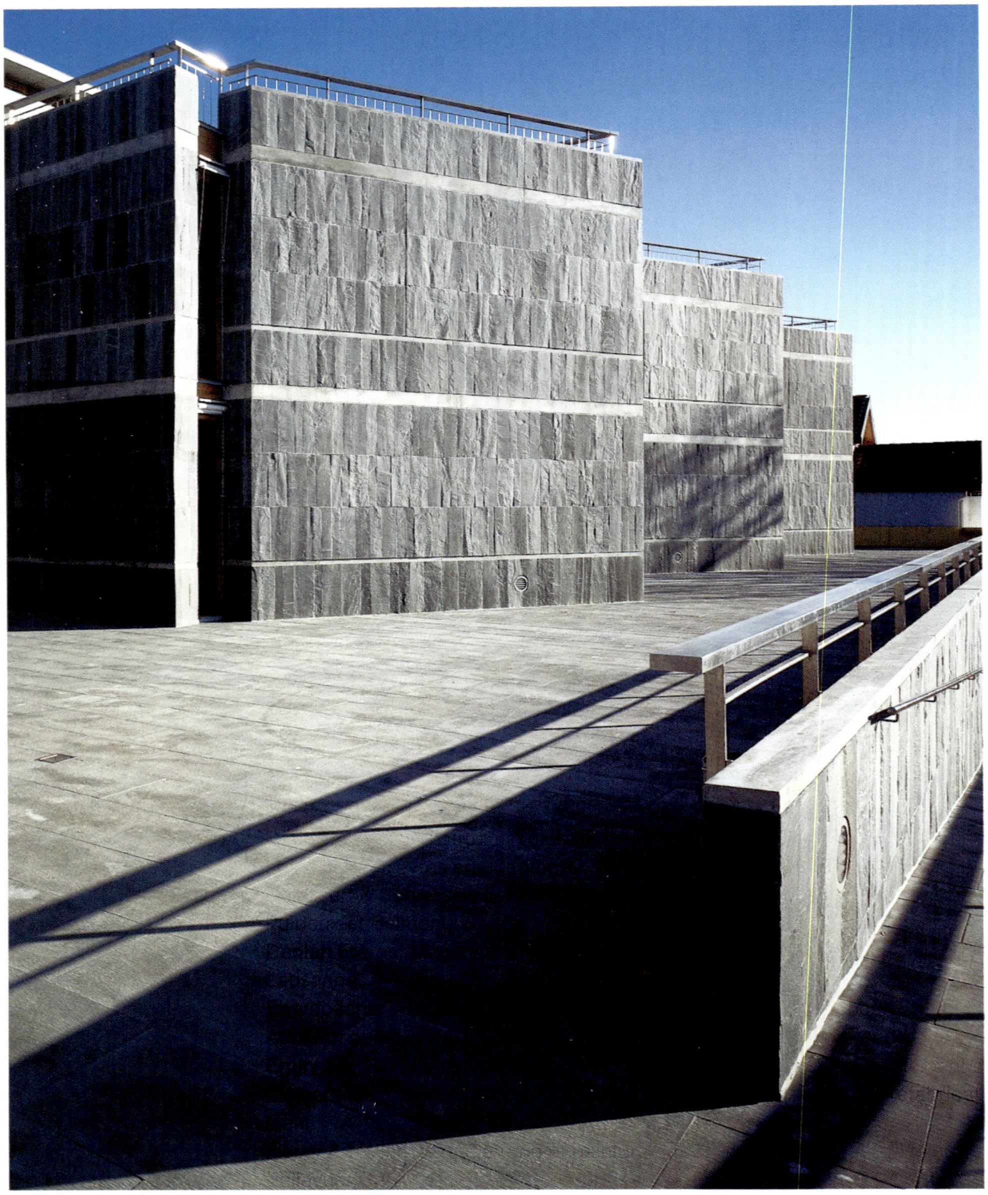

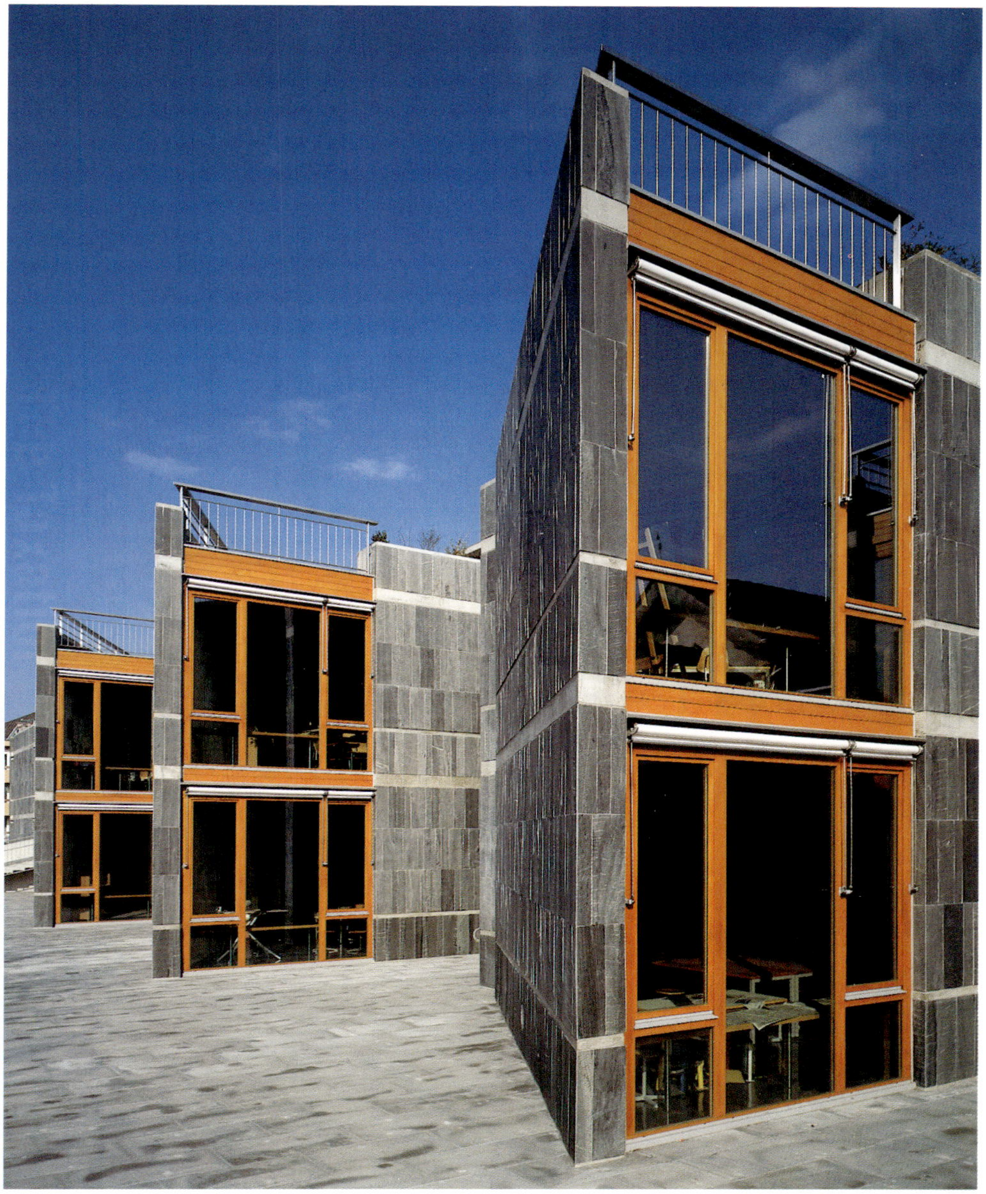

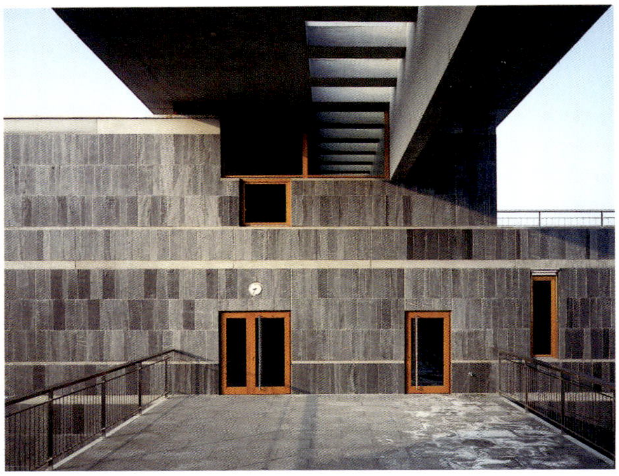

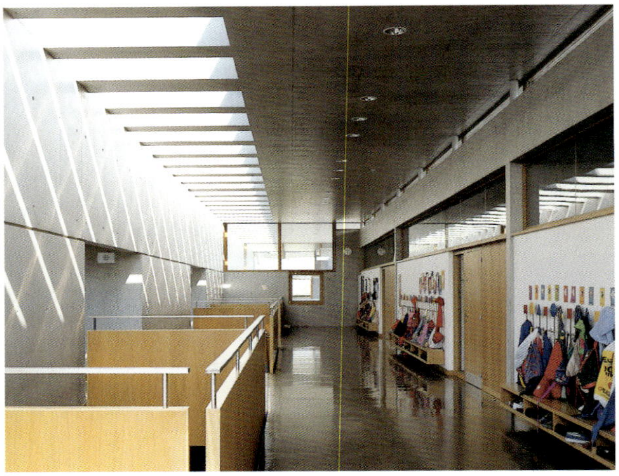

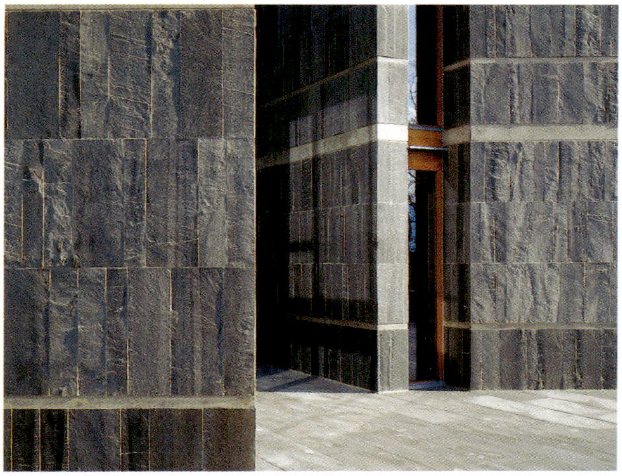
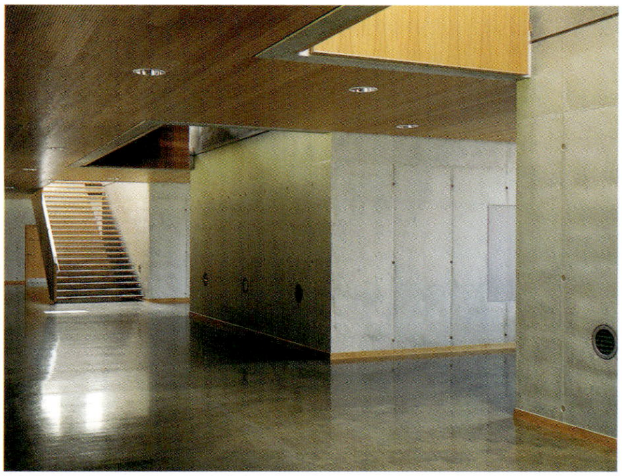

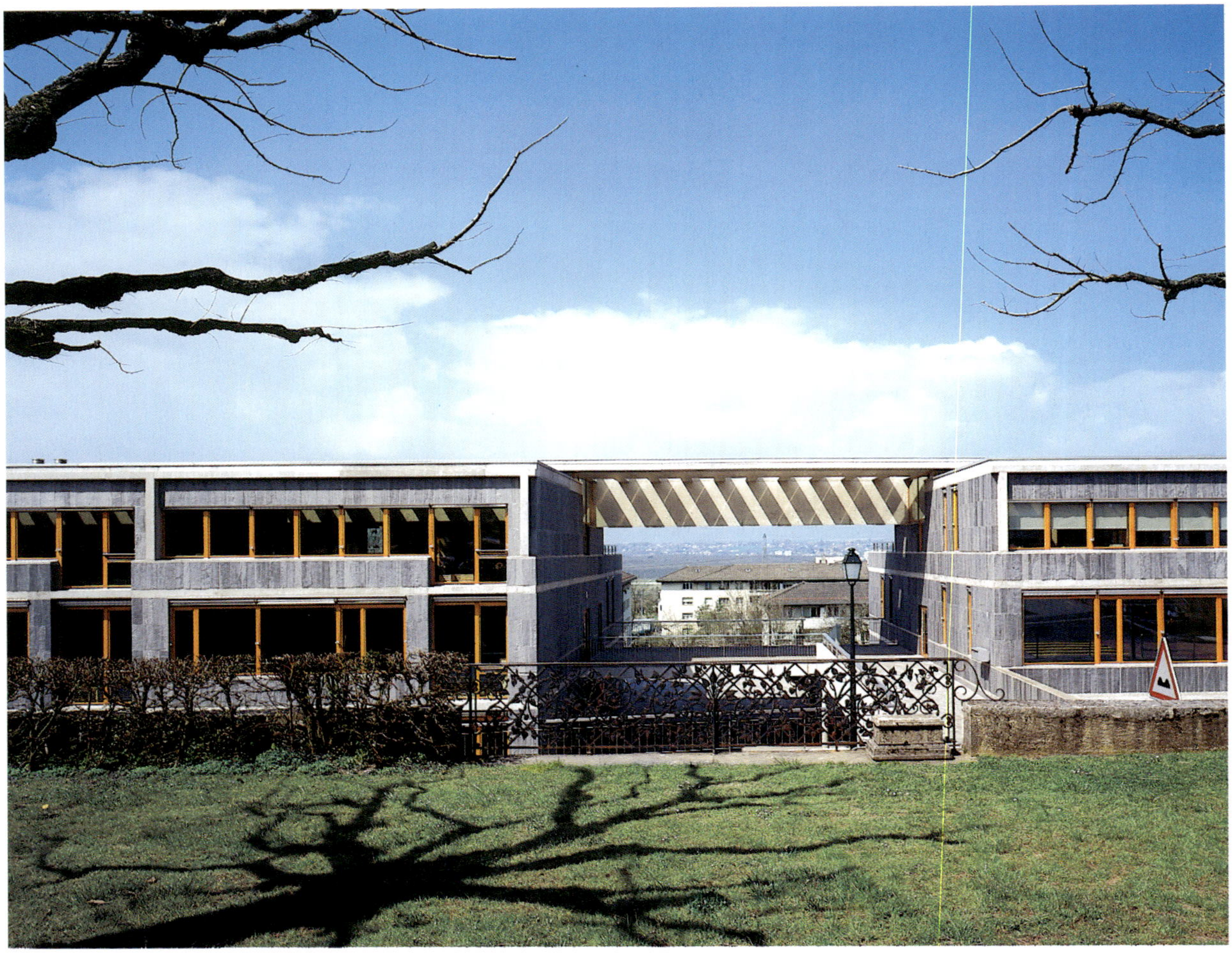

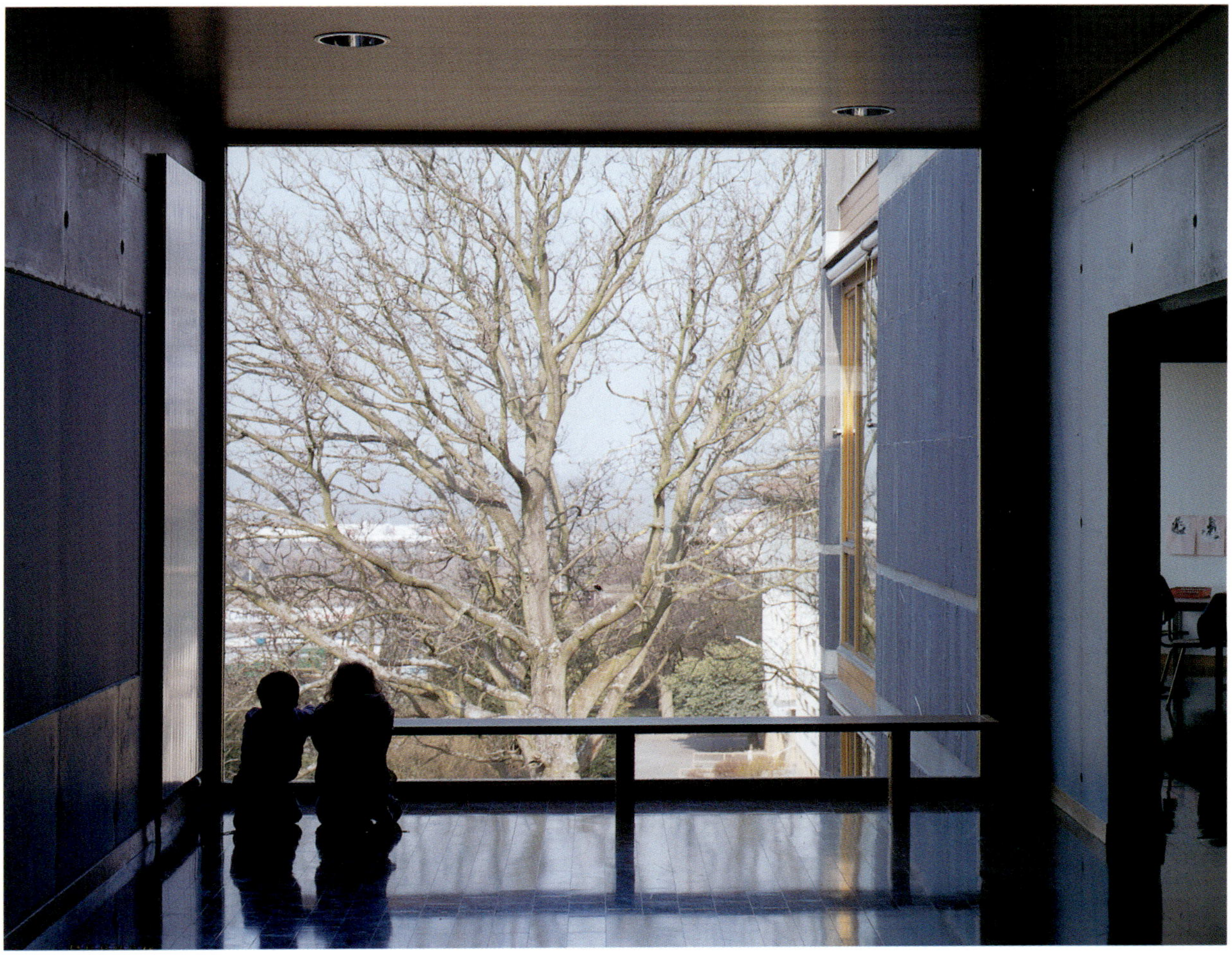

78   Mv 1930 1912   .85

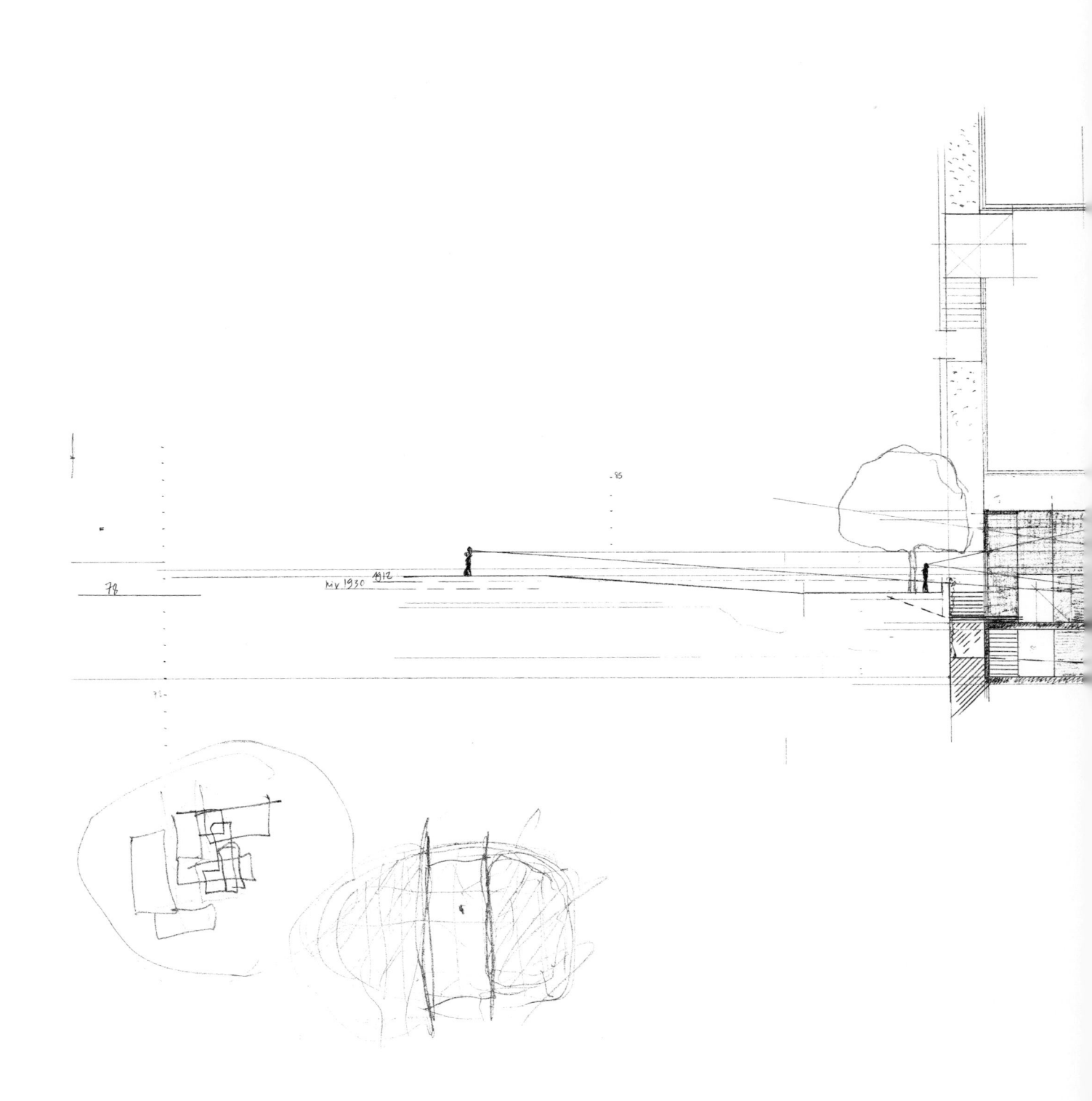

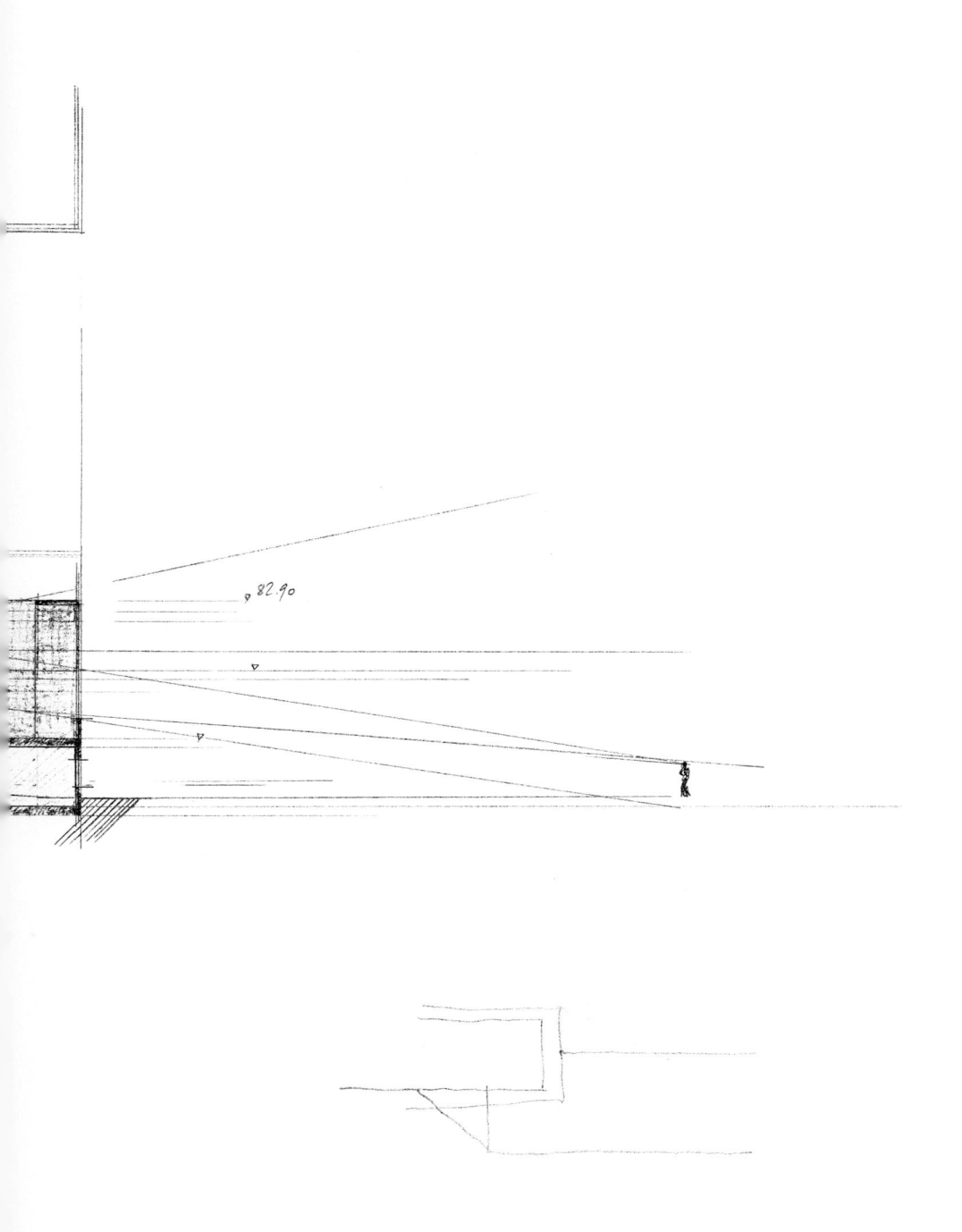

PULLY

PULLY

The school of Chamblandes at Pully near Lausanne comprises two buildings constructed in 1912 on an artificial esplanade flanked by a high wall which rises above a meadow and the lake. Its extension groups the new classrooms in a single, separate building, detached from the wall and at a lower level. The building, in this lower garden, is added to the two others, emphasizing the fluidity of space on the esplanade, where lateral views from one building to another are not only preserved but accentuated. The wall of yellow quartzite in which the stones and openings are inserted with the aim of disrupting its scale and making it no more than the north wall of the volume, opens on to a large transverse hall which allows a view of the lake's surface from the entrance porch of the complex. The slabs, extended by the marquises, prolong the lake landscape inside the building through an alternation of transparent glass and panels of translucent fibreglass. The aluminum facades are related to nautical technology (carbon fibre embedded in polyester) to form a curtain onto the lake.

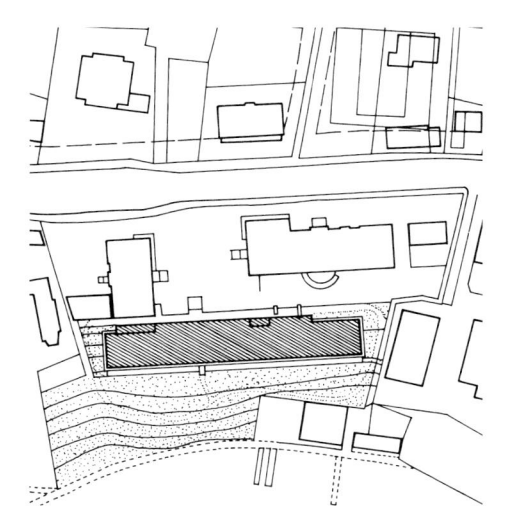

Das Gymnasium von Chamblandes in Pully, nahe bei Lausanne, besteht aus zwei Bauten von 1912, die erhöht über See und Gelände auf einer künstlichen, von einer hohen Mauer gesäumten Plattform liegen. Sein neuer Erweiterungsbau präsentiert sich als autonomes Einzelvolumen, das von der Mauer abgelöst weiter unten im Gelände steht. Von seiner Lage im unteren Gartenteil her, ergänzt das Gebäude die beiden Vorhandenen und betont das Fließende des Plattformraums, die dortigen Blickperspektiven von einem Volumen aufs andere nicht nur bewahrend, sondern noch unterstreichend. Die Wand aus gelbem Quarzit, in die Steine und Öffnungen so eingefügt sind, daß ihr die Mächtigkeit genommen wird und sie als schlichte Nordwand des Volumens erscheinen kann, öffnet sich auf eine großzügige, durchgehende Halle hin. Schon vom Eingangsportal her wird die Sicht auf den See freigegeben. Die Bodenplatten sind in den Außenraum gezogen und verlängern, zusammen mit dem Wechselspiel von durchsichtigem Glas und durchscheinenden Glasfaserplatten, die Seelandschaft ins Innere hinein. Die Aluminiumfassaden verbinden sich mit den Anleihen aus der Schiffsbautechnologie (die Glasfaserplatten bestehen aus in Polyester gegossenen Kohlenstoffdrähten) und bilden zusammen einen Vorhang zum See hin.

55

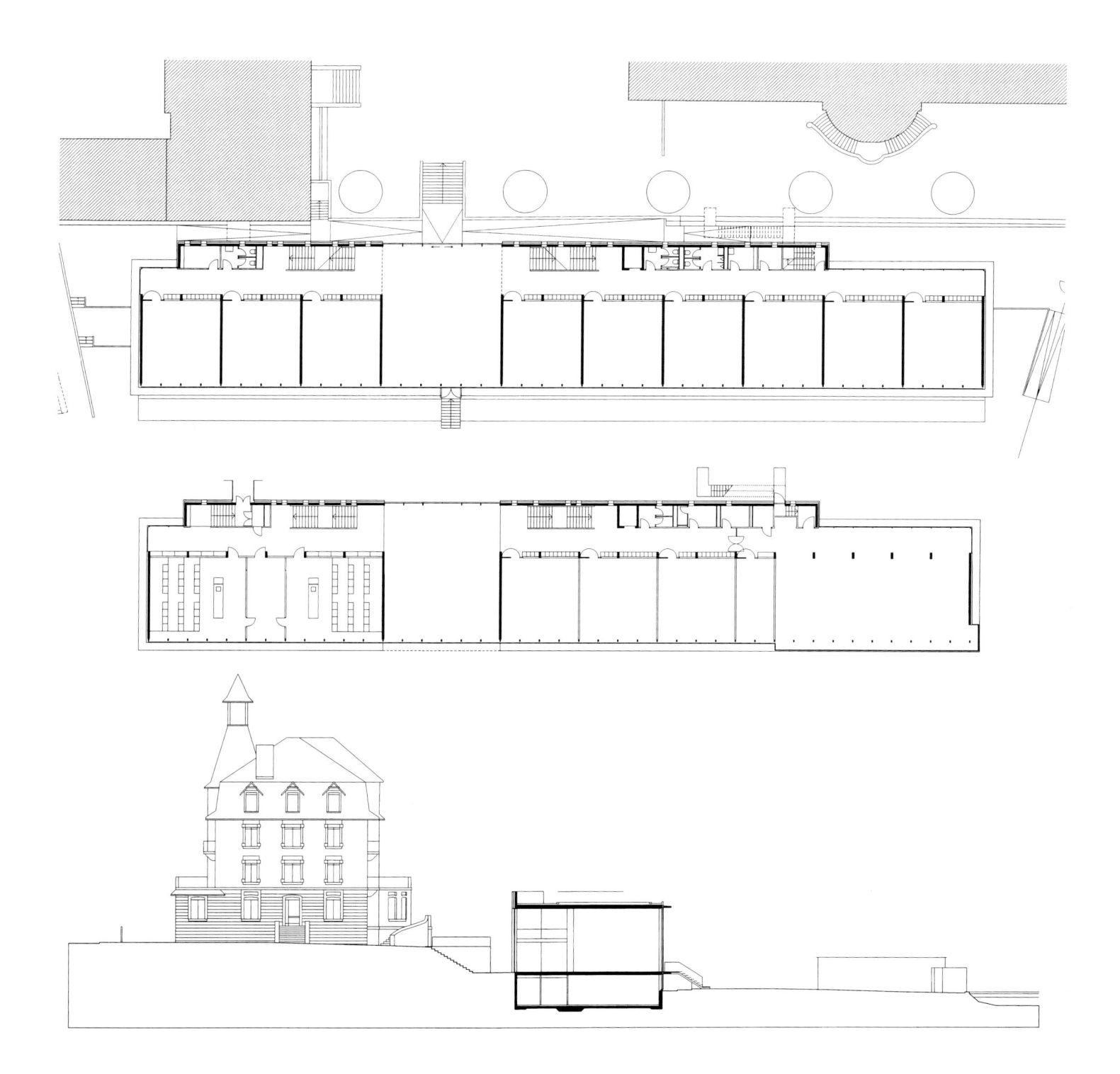

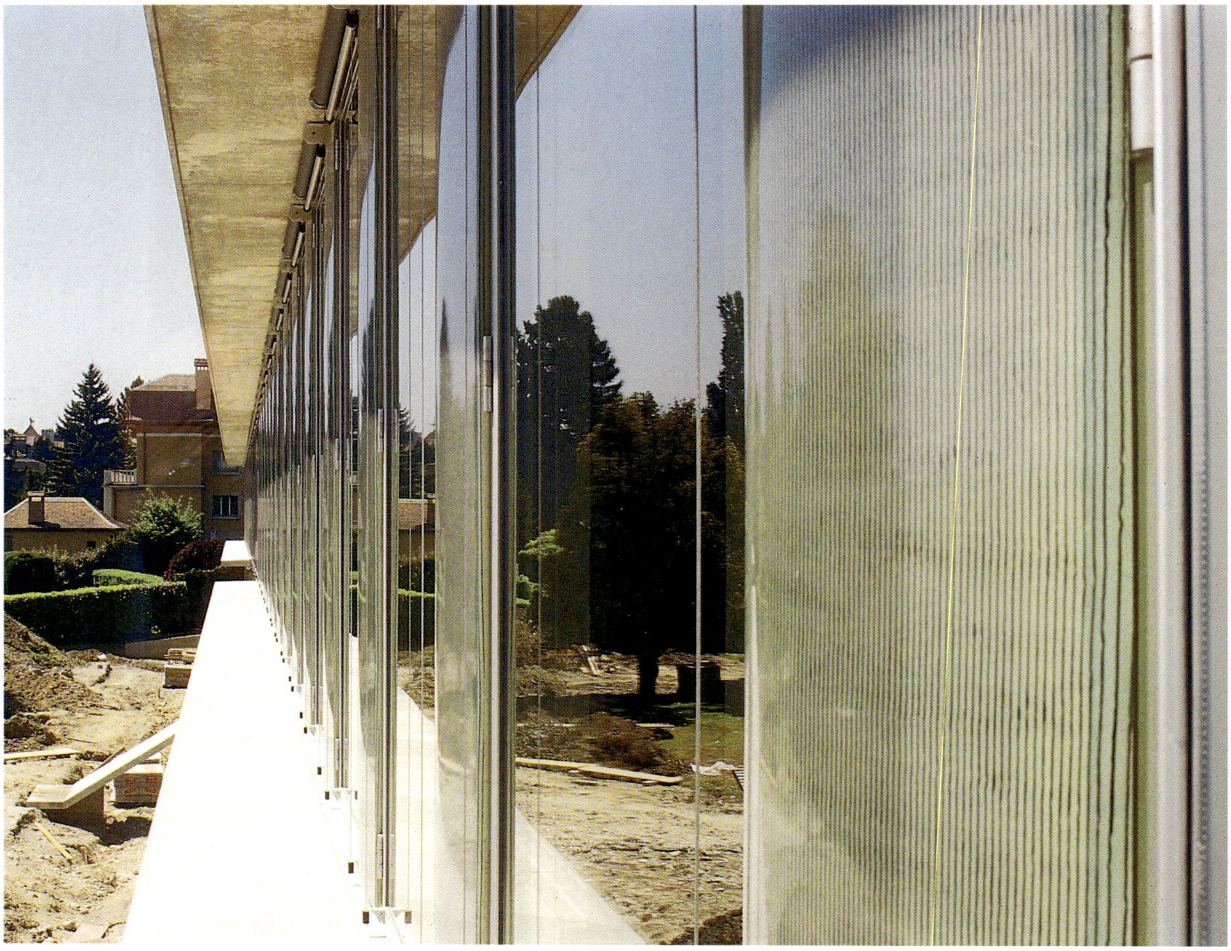

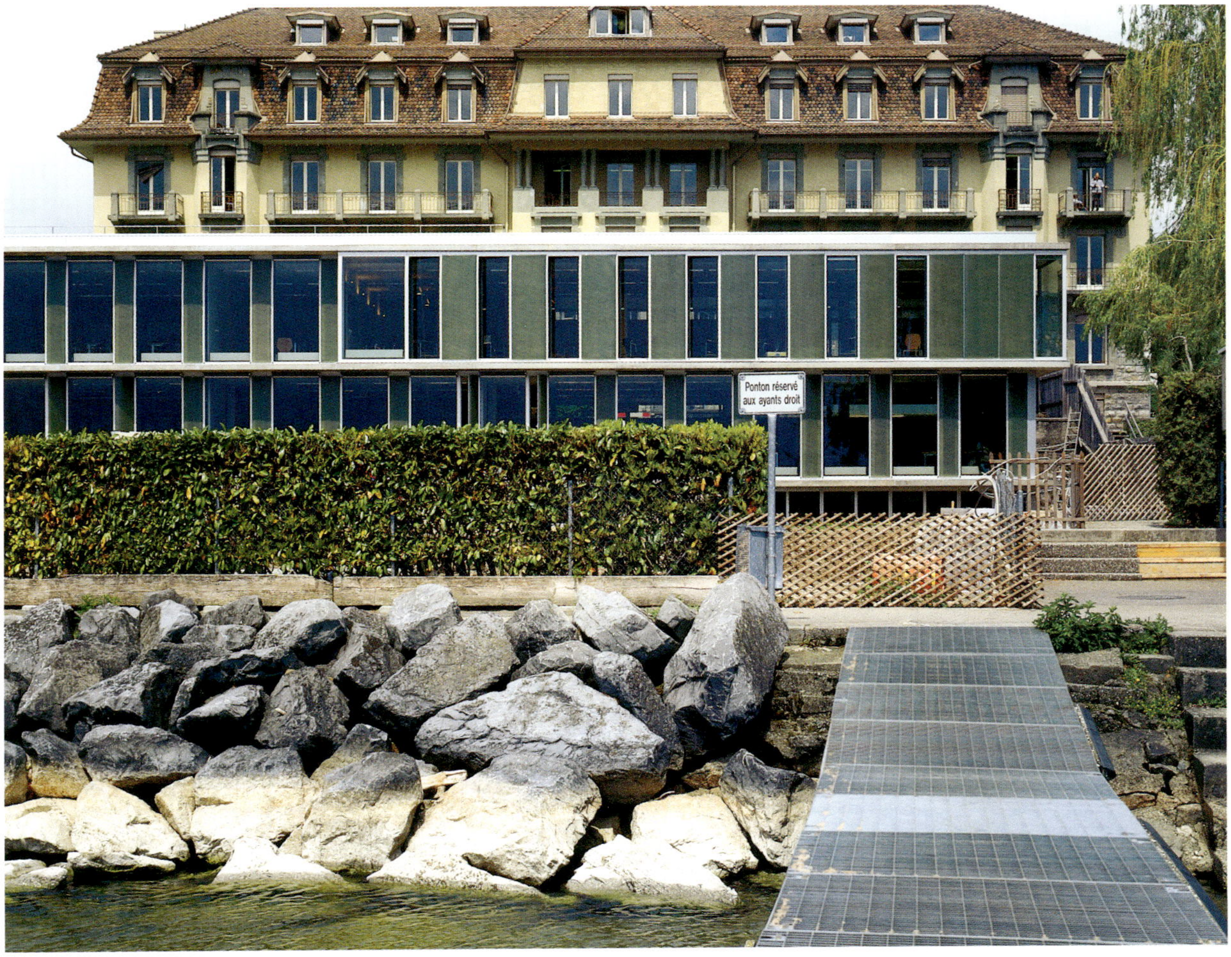
Ponton réservé
aux ayants droit

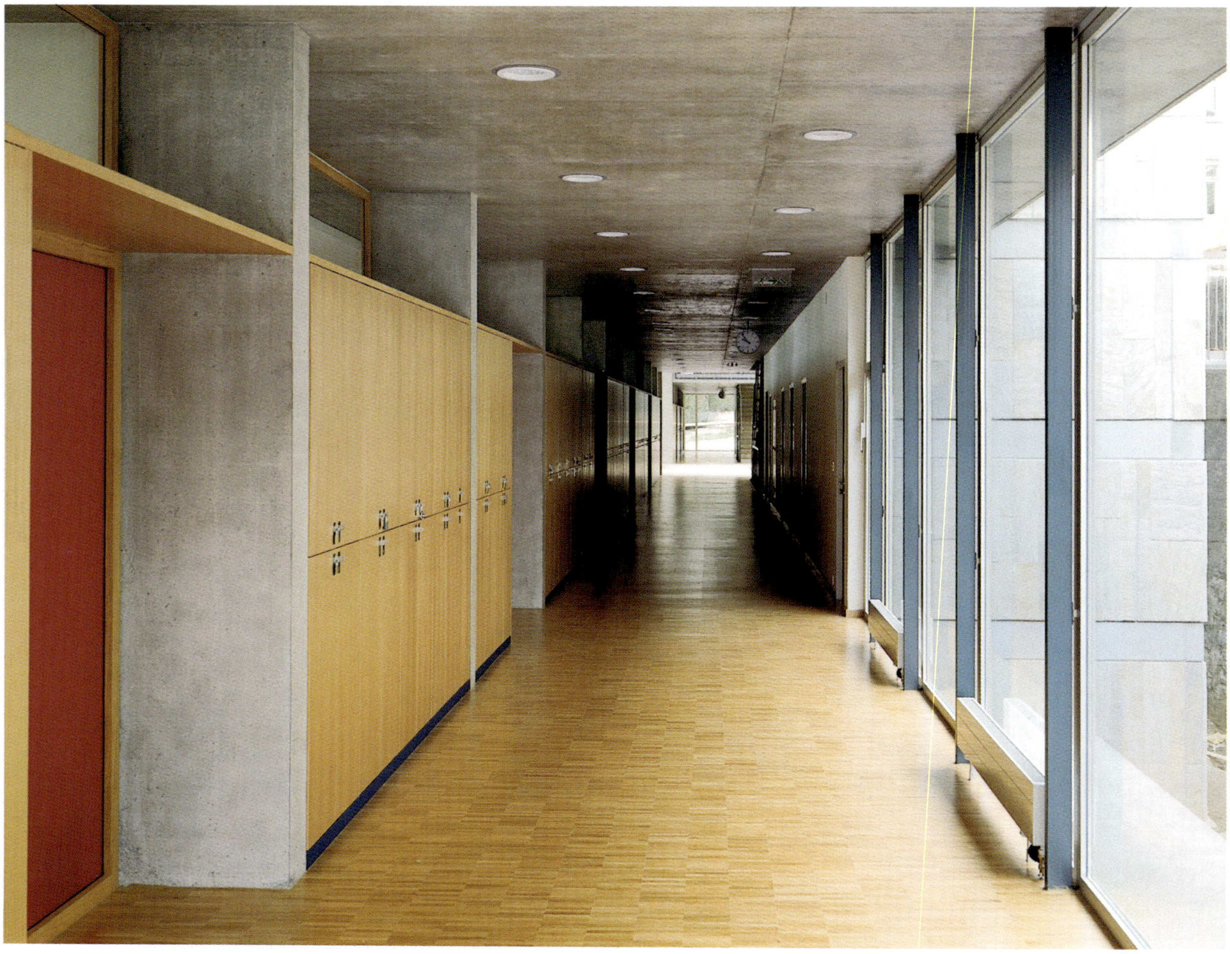

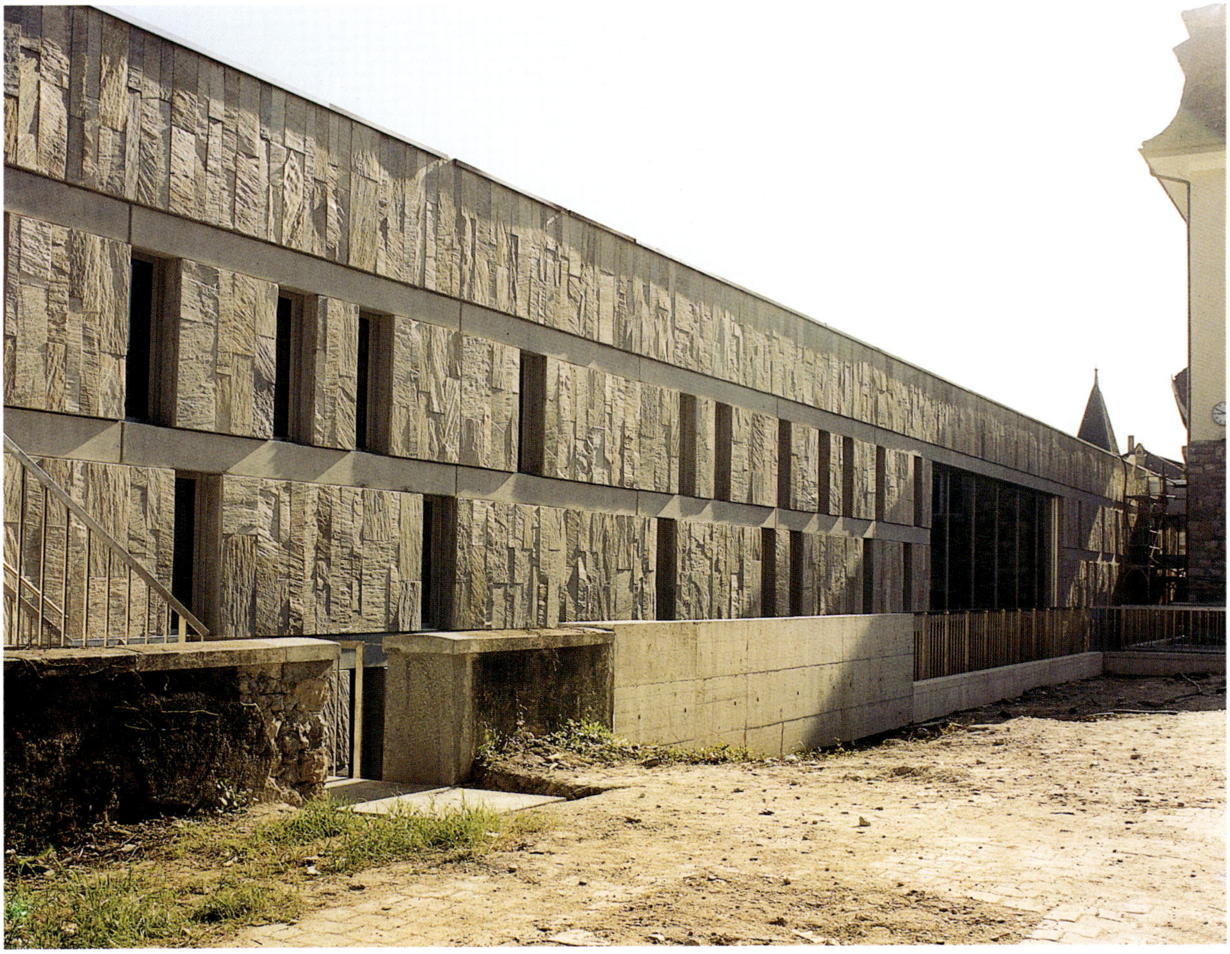

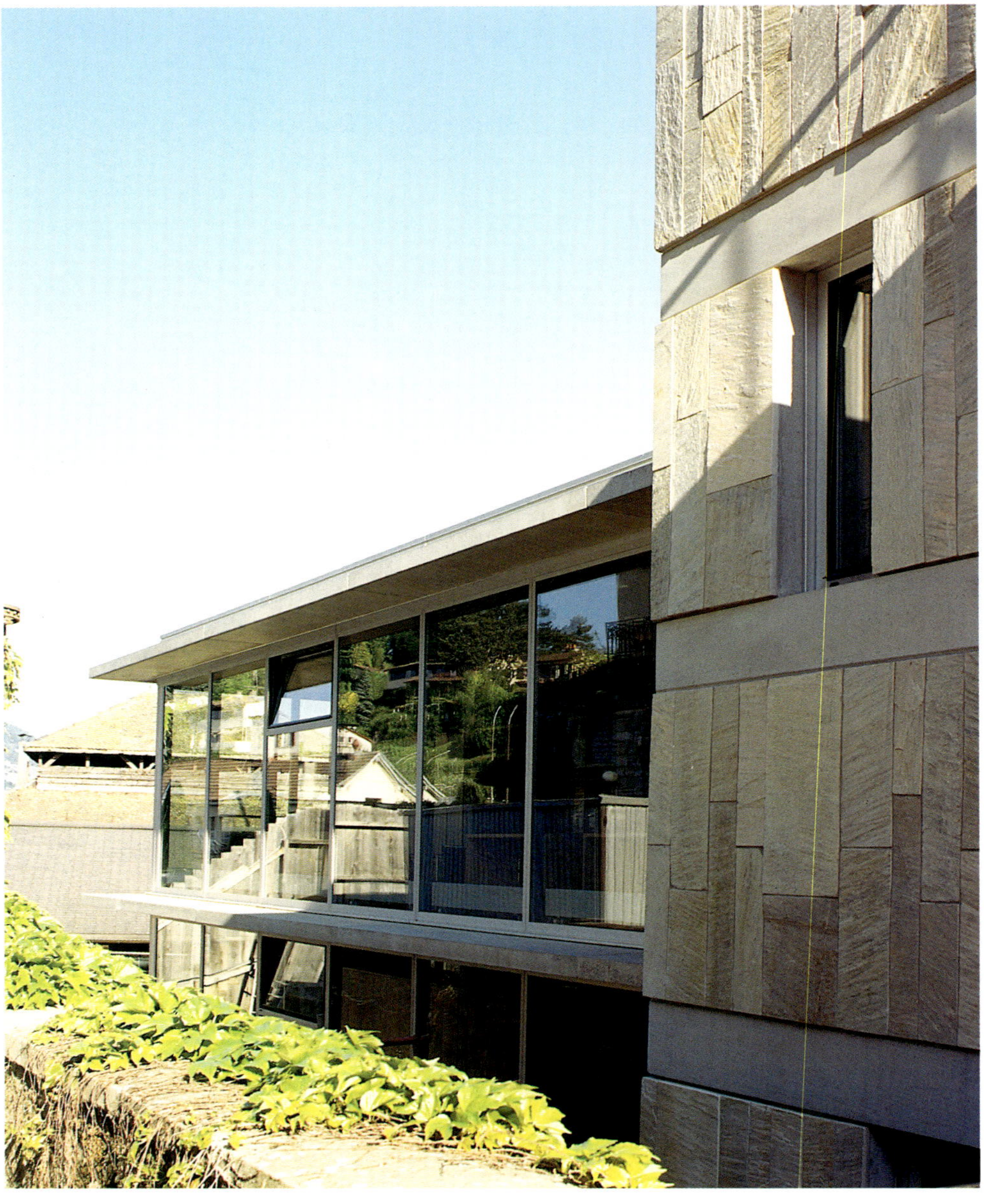

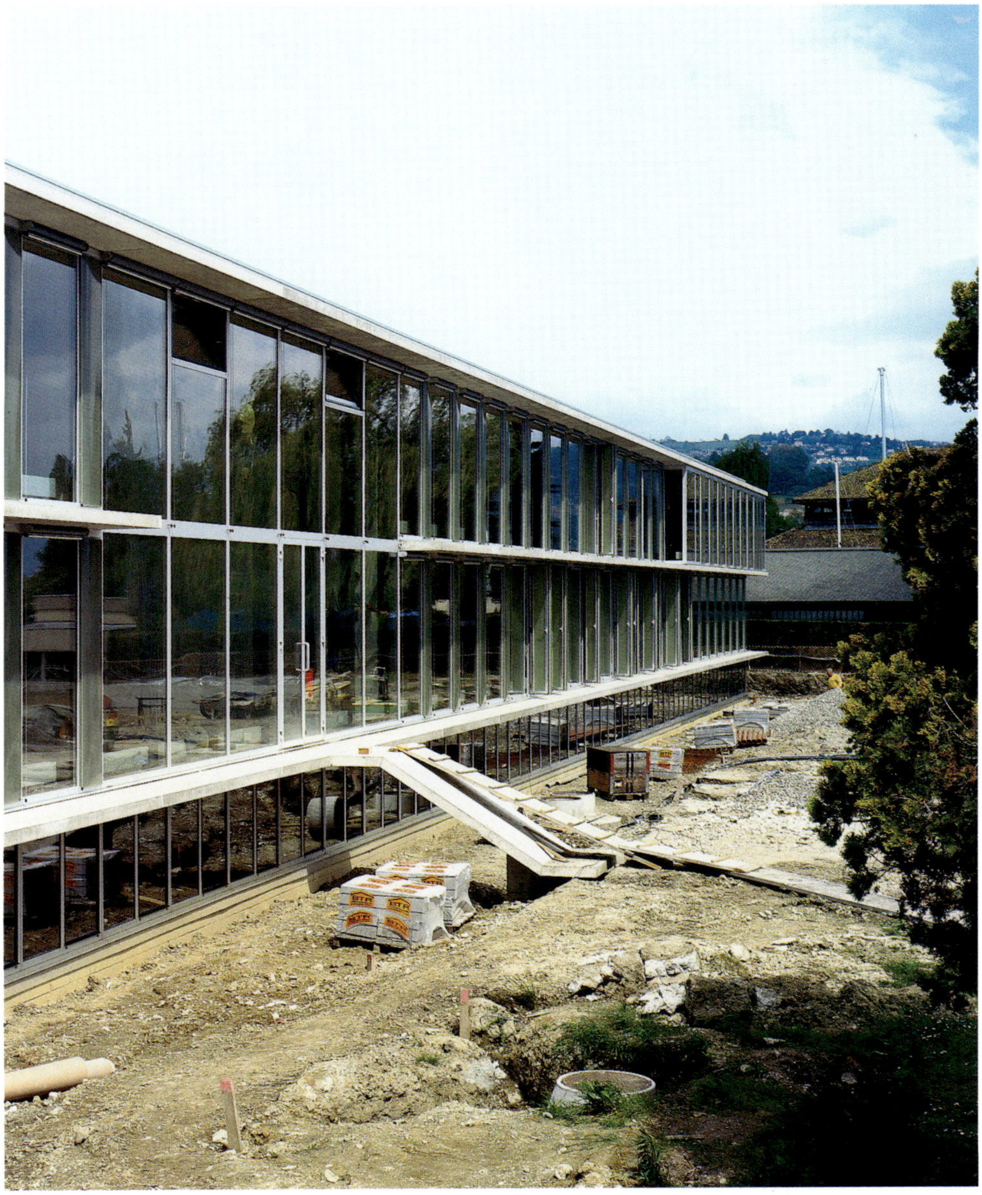

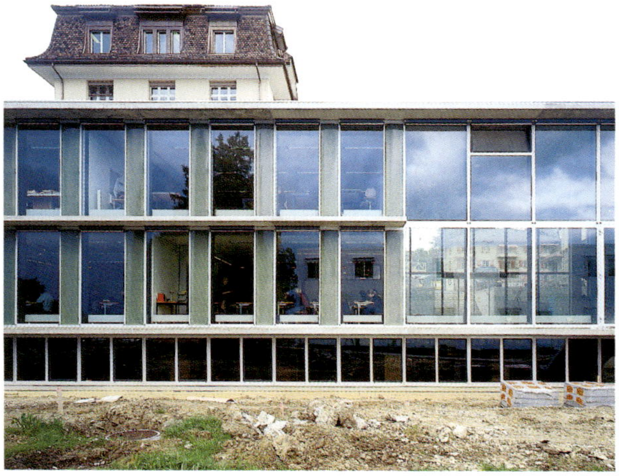
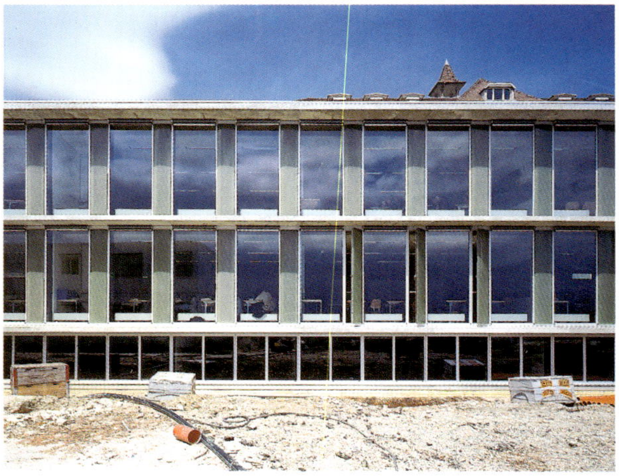
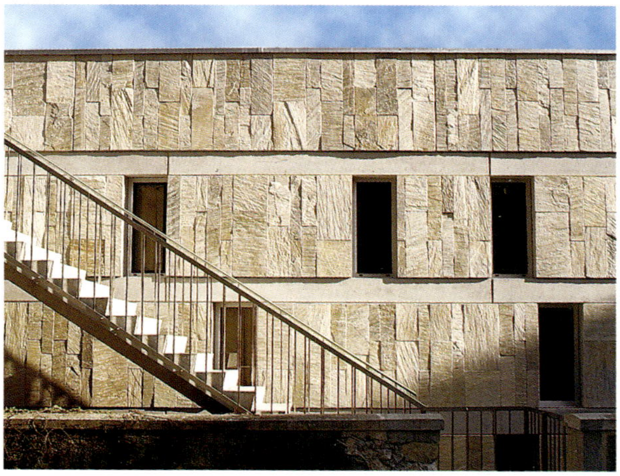
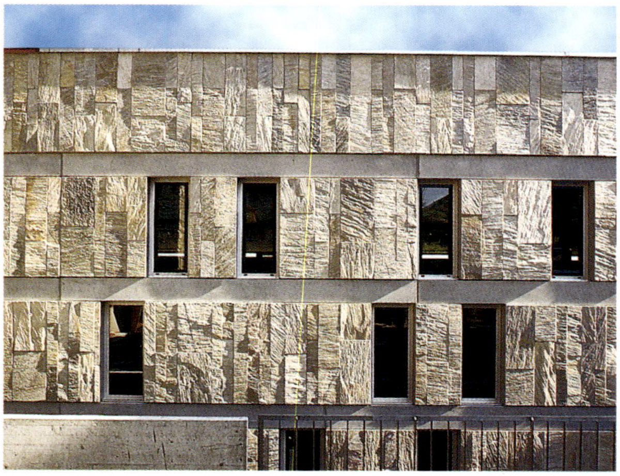

63

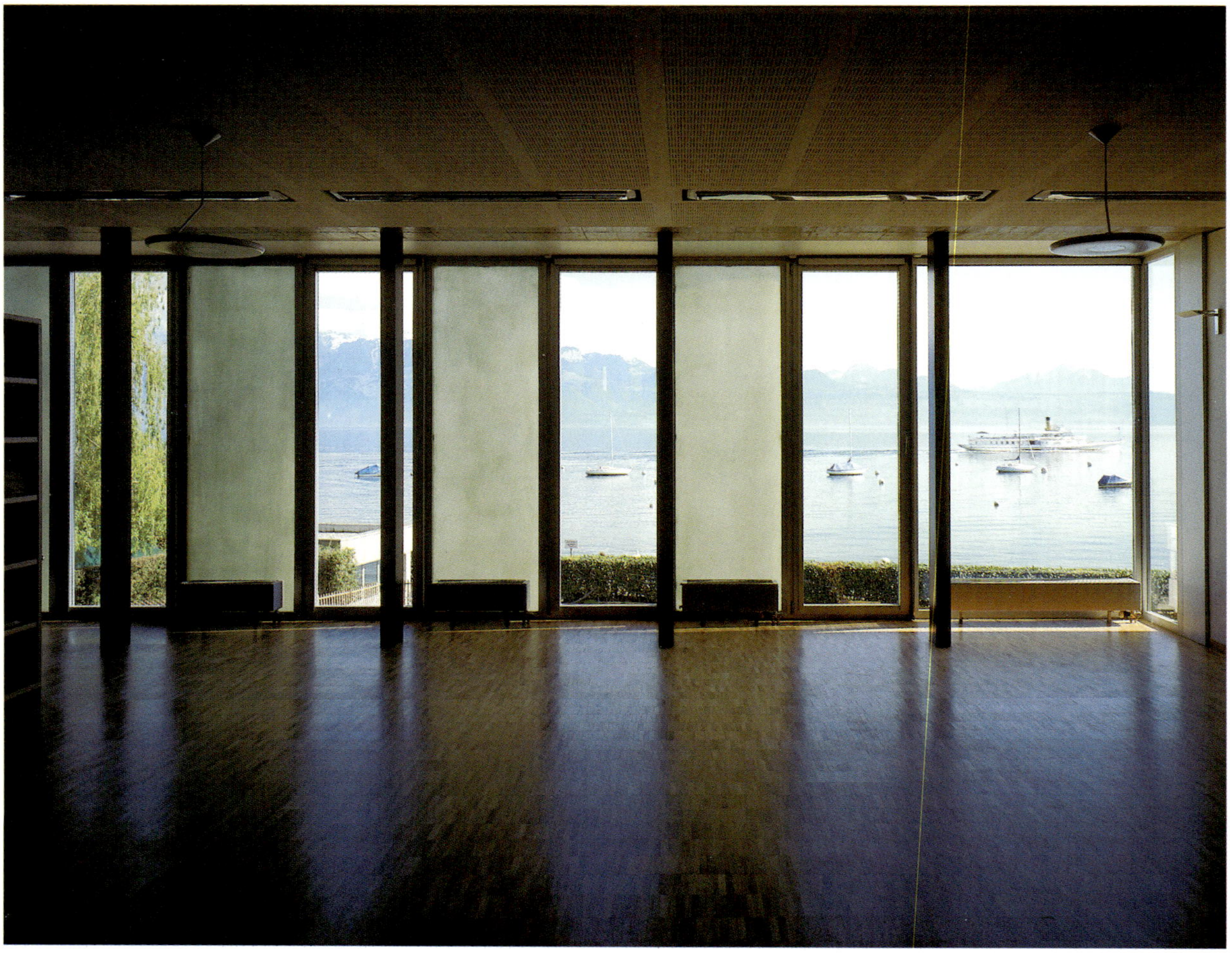

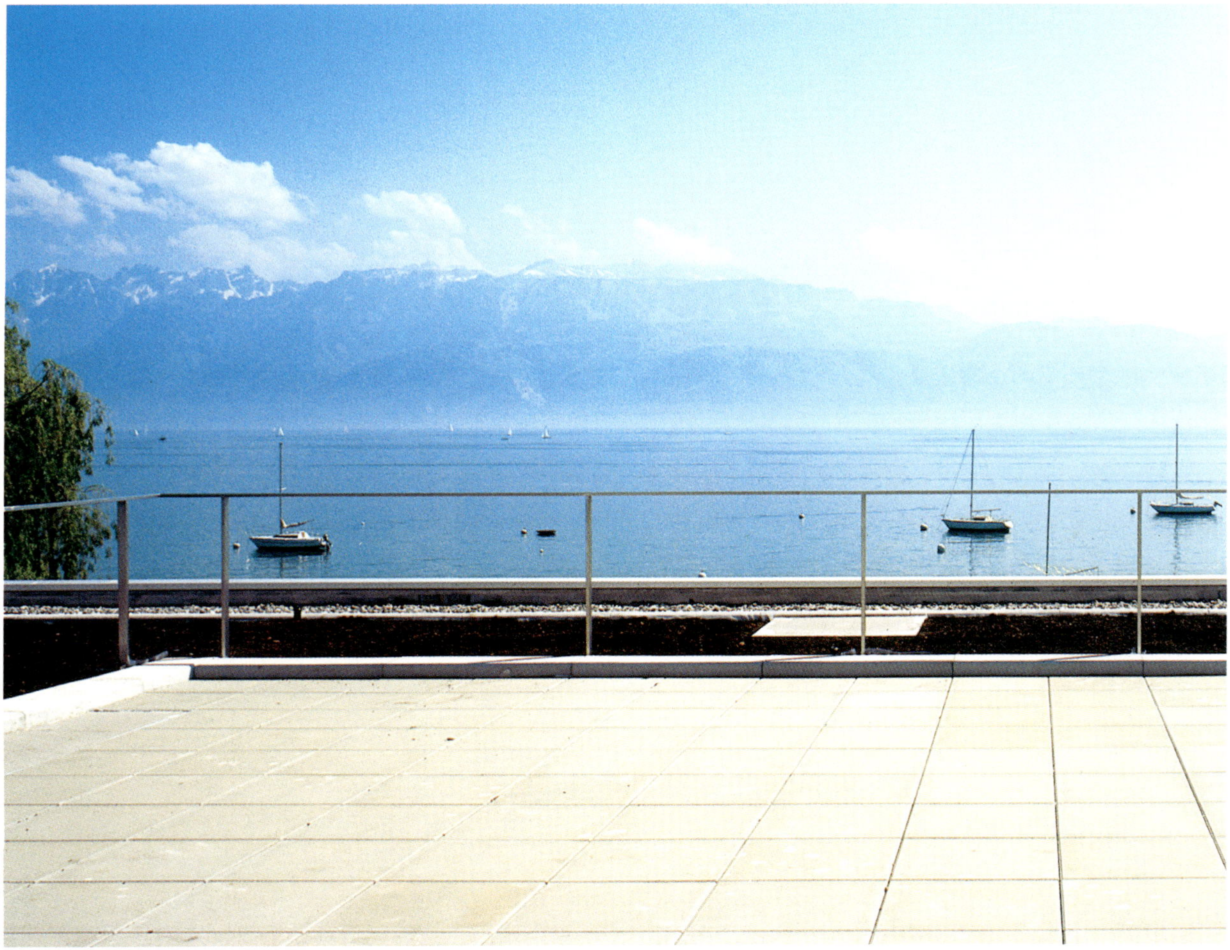

volet

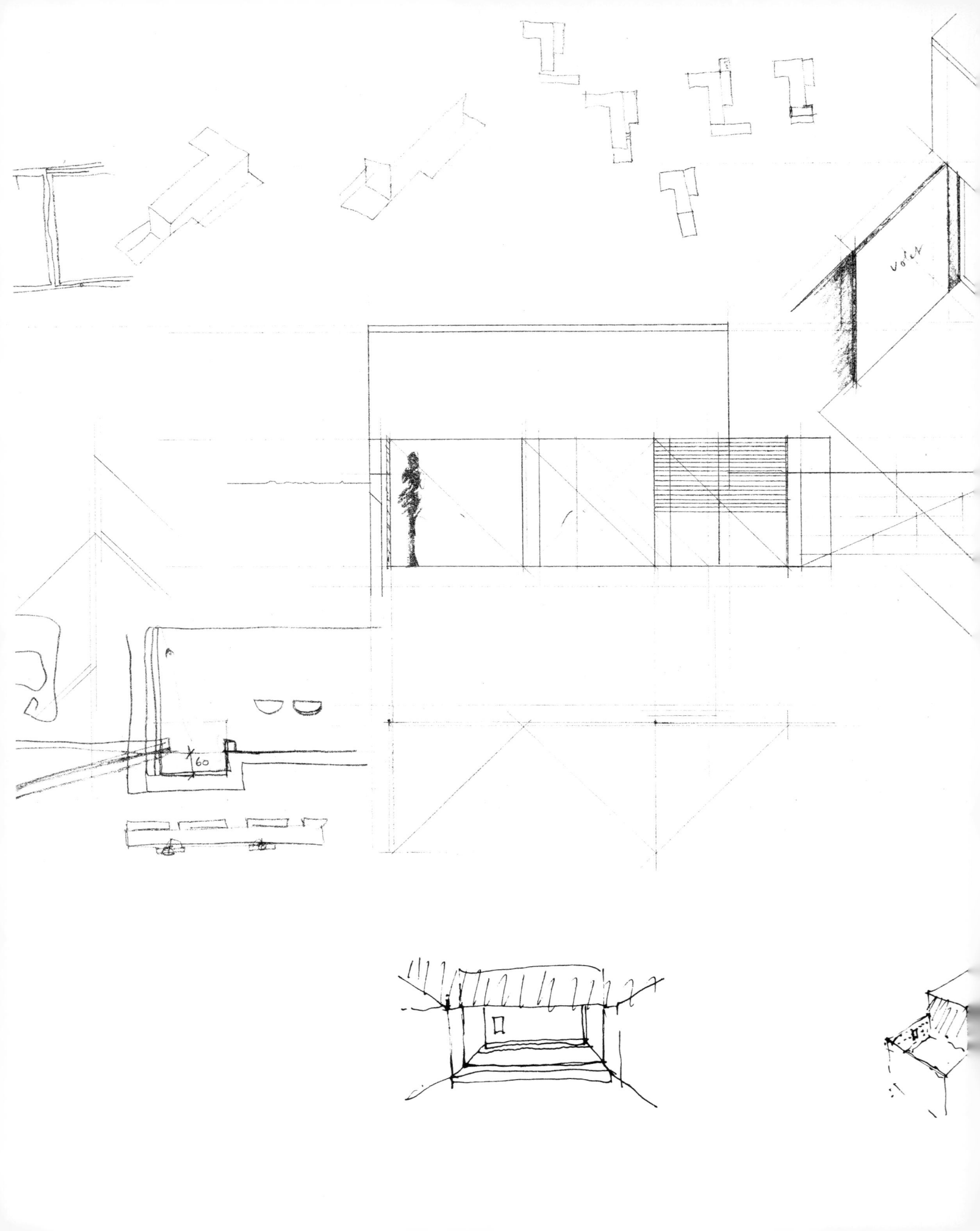

CUGY

CUGY

The Gringet residence at Cugy, in the periphery of Lausanne, is located, half-buried, in the garden of an existing family house typical of villa developments of the 1960s. The site is surrounded by hedges which enclose the exterior space like a large room open to the sky. The ground floor of the existing building, raised 160 cm above ground level, defines a horizon line opening on to the landscape of the immediate vicinity. The new house in concrete, is built below this eye reference level, offering no view except that of its own walls juxtaposed to the greens of lawn and hedges. The management of proportion, of light and of material plays on the idea of this 'block of coal' buried in and emerging from the ground. Its colour (three superimposed mineral undercoats – red, blue and black) represents both the black of a waterproofing membrane and an absence of colour contrasting to the colours of the garden. The interior is white, intimate and neutral, with only domestic objects standing out.

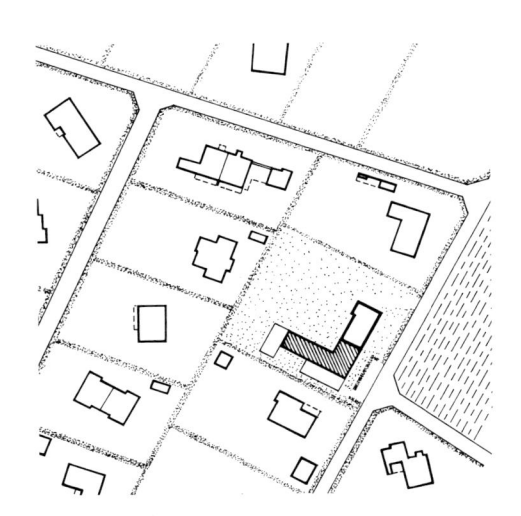

Das Haus Gringet, im nicht weit von Lausanne entfernten Cugy liegt, halbwegs versenkt unter die Erdoberfläche, im Garten eines bestehenden Einfamilienhauses, das ein typisches Beispiel für den Villenbau der 60er Jahre ist. Das Grundstück ist von Hecken umgeben, wodurch der Außenraum geschlossen wirkt wie ein großes Zimmer ohne Decke. Das Erdgeschoß des bestehenden Hauses, das 1,60 m über dem Erdboden erhöht liegt, gibt eine Blicklinie vor, die auf das Unausgeprägte der nahen Umgebung gerichtet ist. Das neue Haus aus Beton steht unterhalb dieser Linie; es bietet keine andere Sicht als die auf seine eigenen Wände, die dem Grün des Rasens und der Hecken gegenübergestellt sind. Proportionen, Licht und Materialien gestalten sich im Spiel um diesen «Kohle-Block», der in den Erdboden versinkt und wieder auftaucht. Seine Farbe (Überlagerung der drei Mineralfarben rot, blau und schwarz) ist ebenso ein Schwarz der Undurchdringlichkeit wie ein Fehlen von Farbe angesichts der Buntheit des Gartens. Der Innenraum ist weiß, intim und neutral, nur die Einrichtungsgegenstände setzen sich ab.

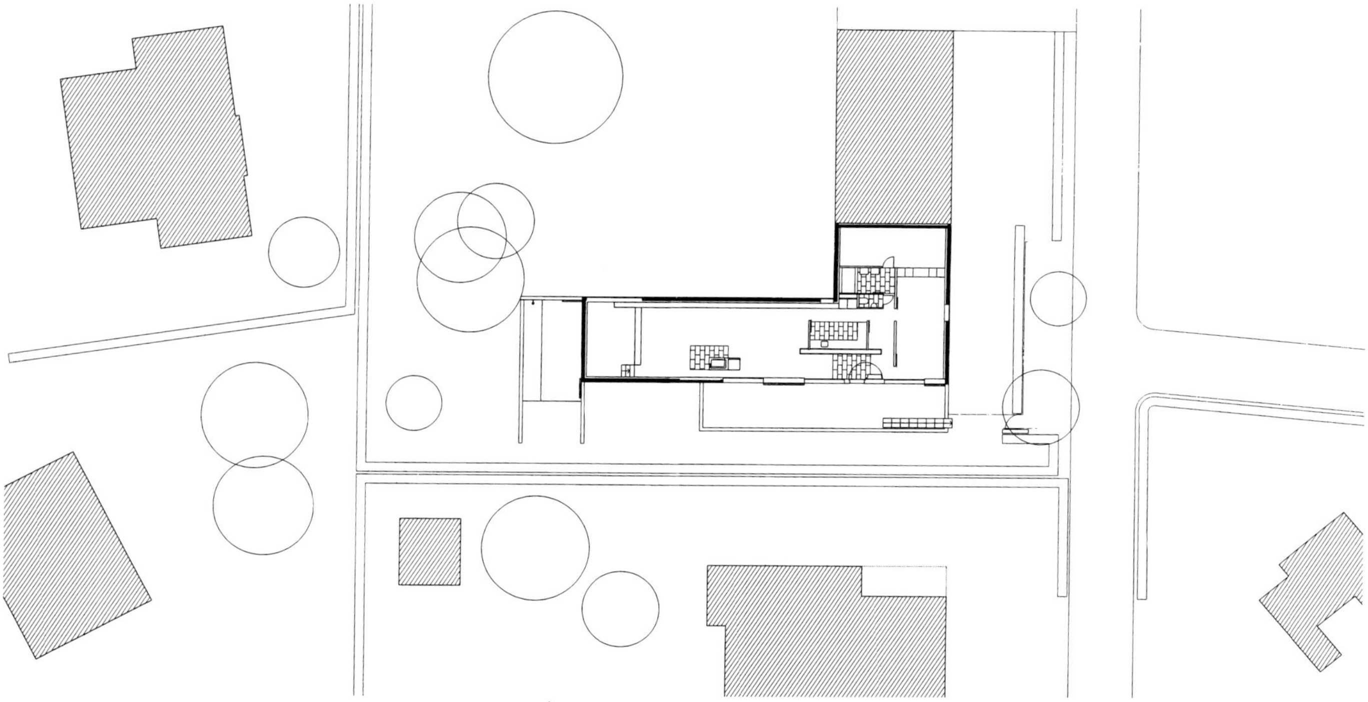

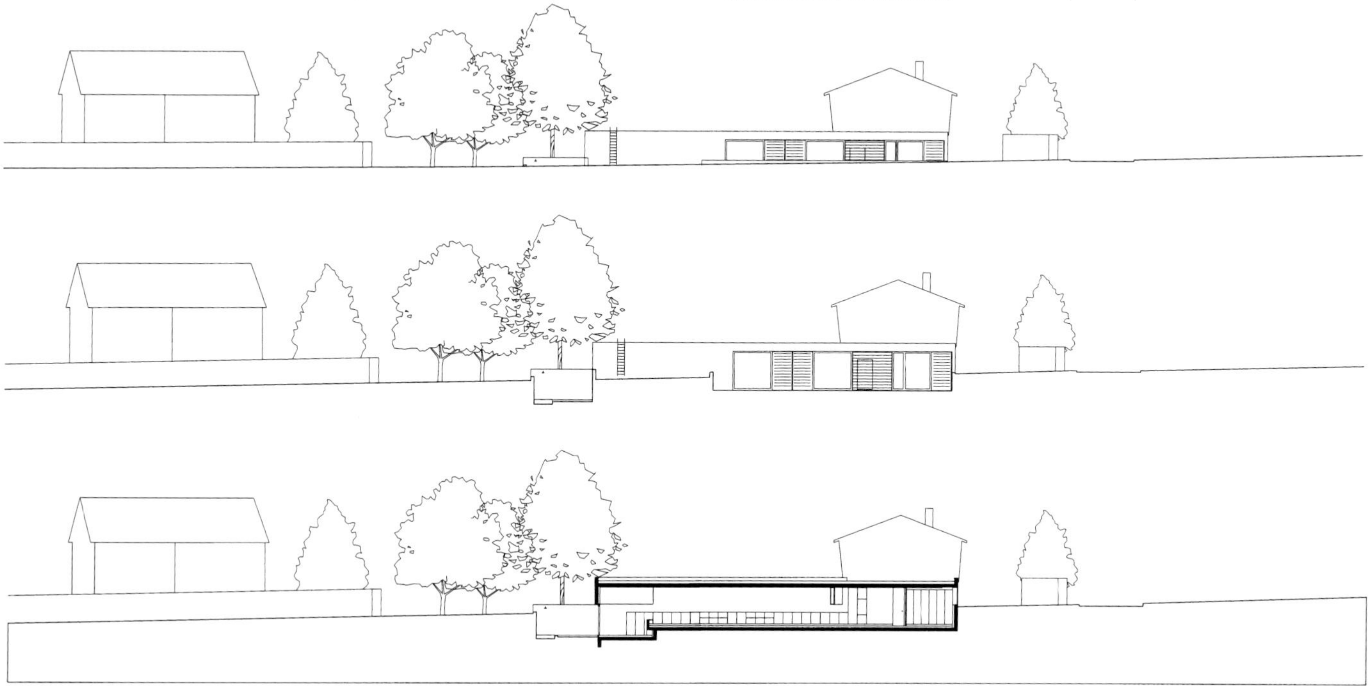

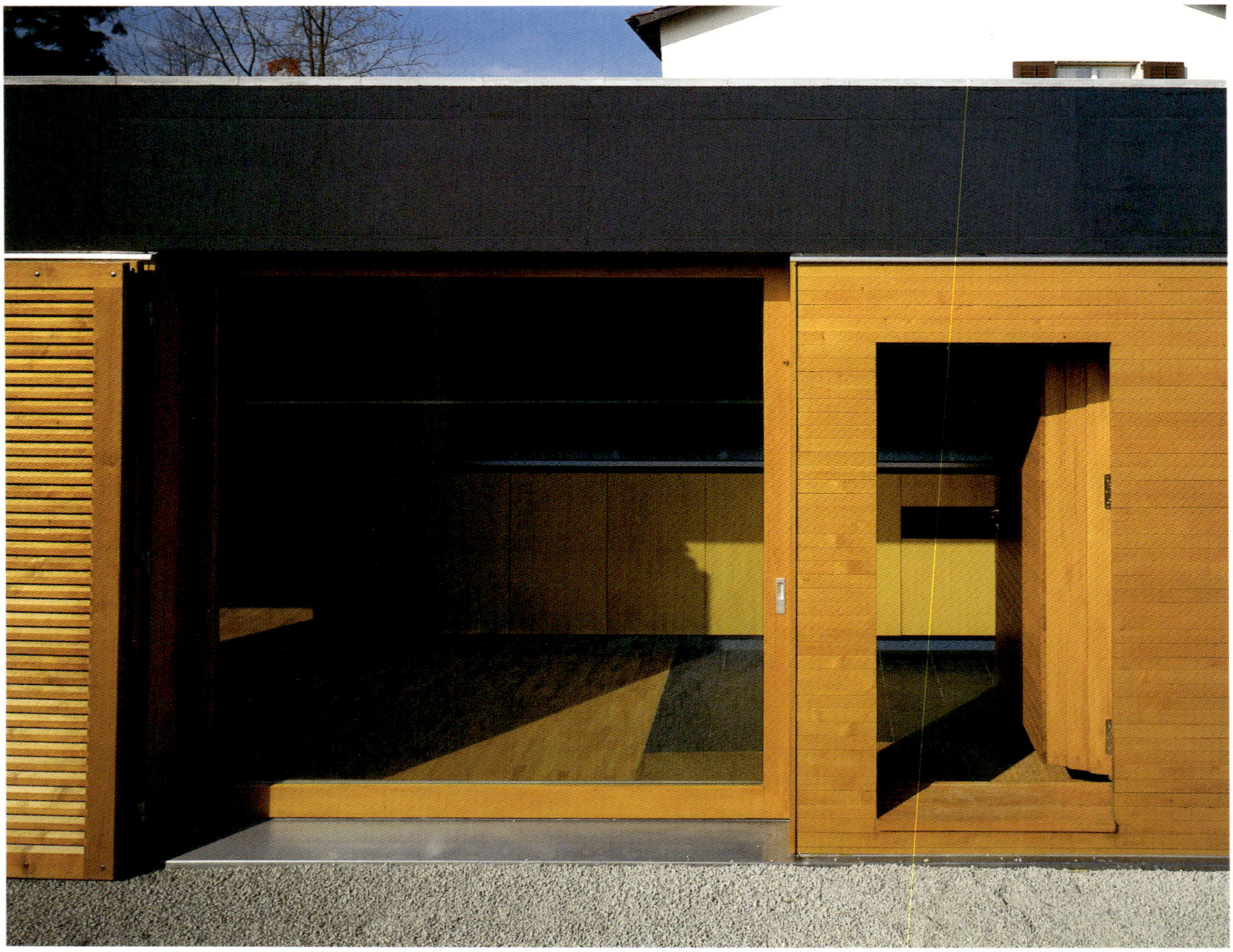

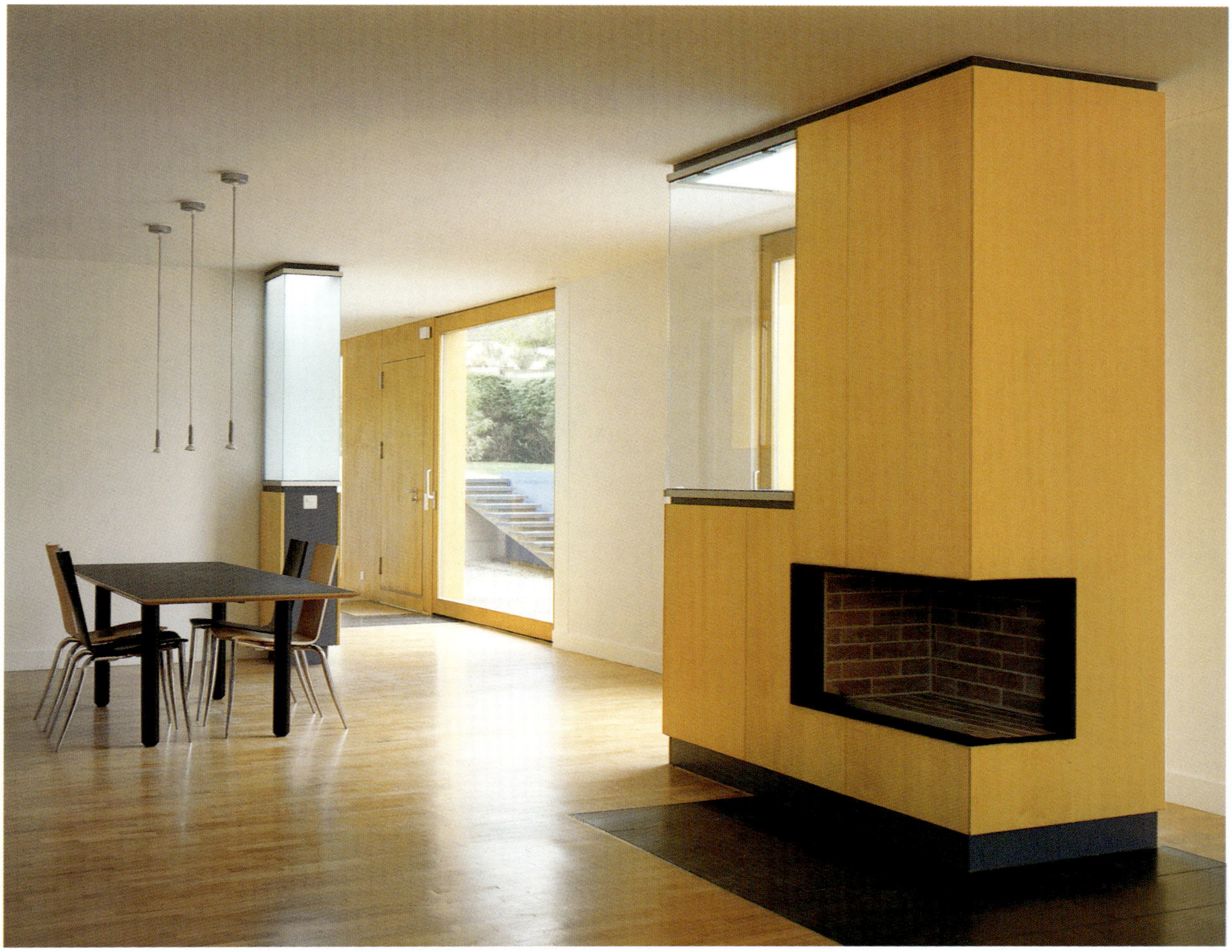

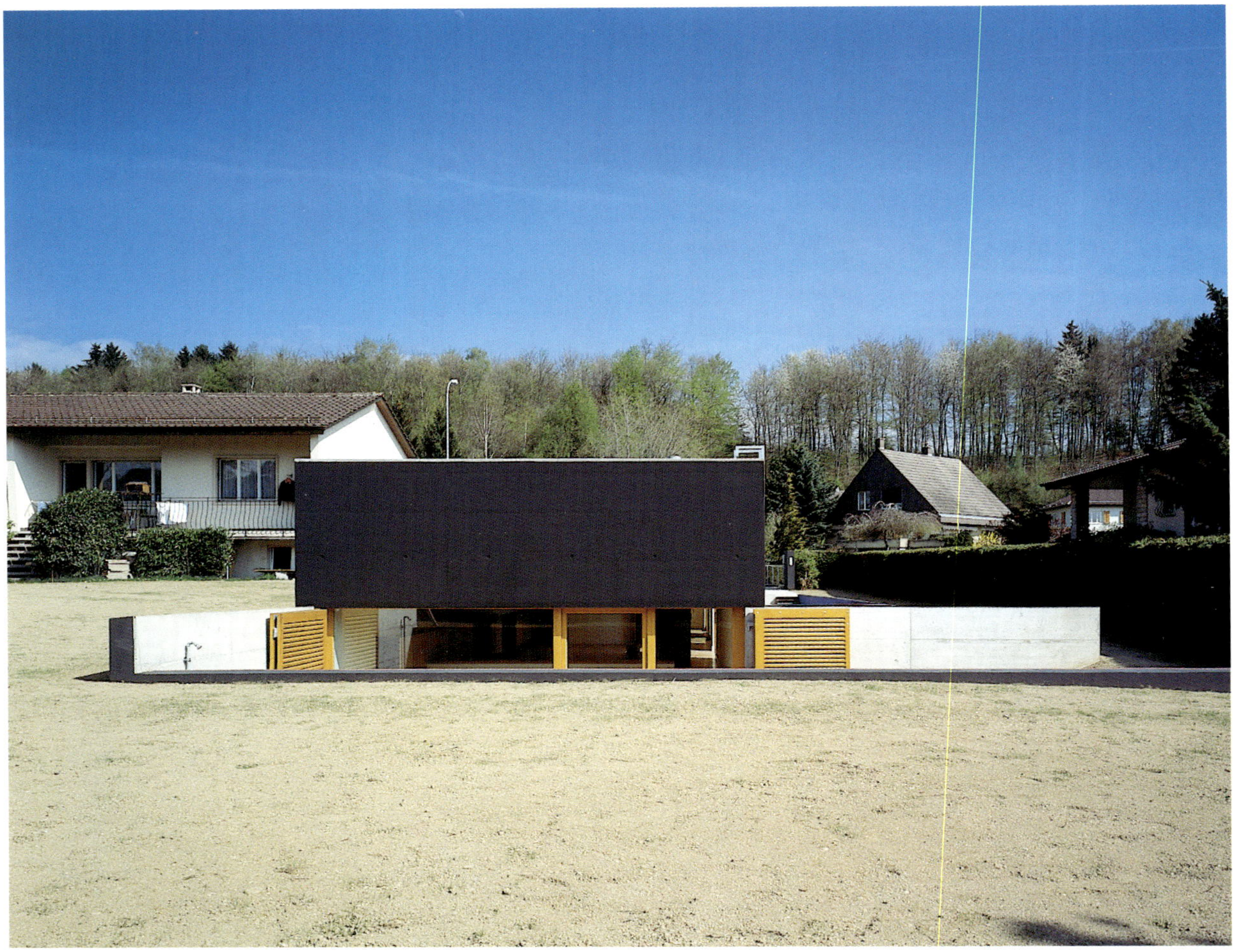

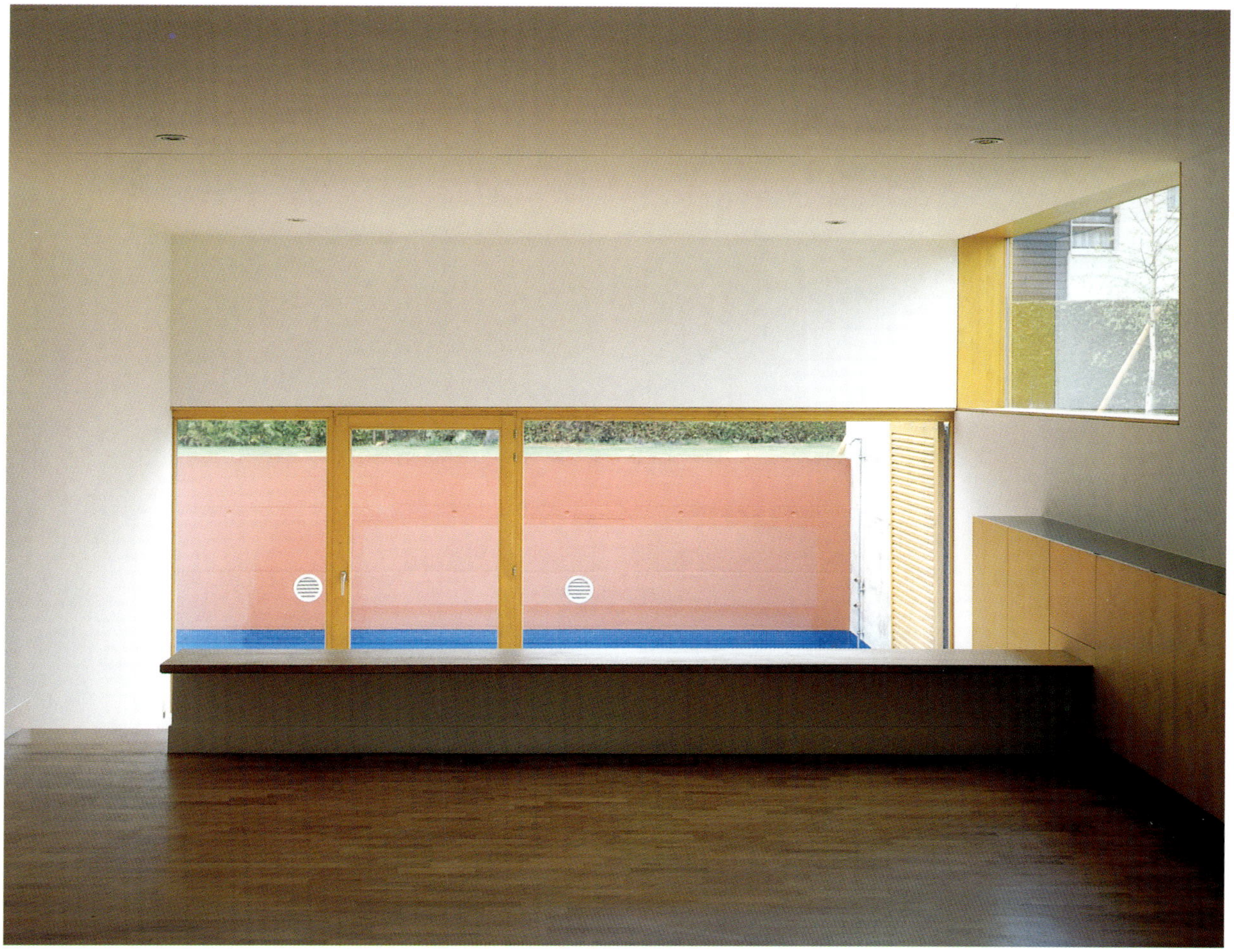

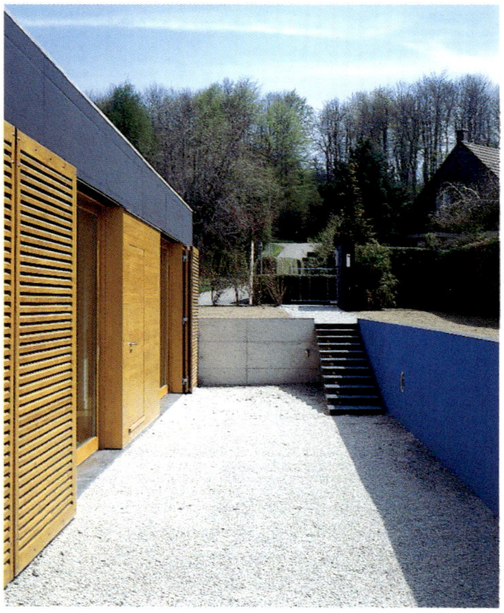

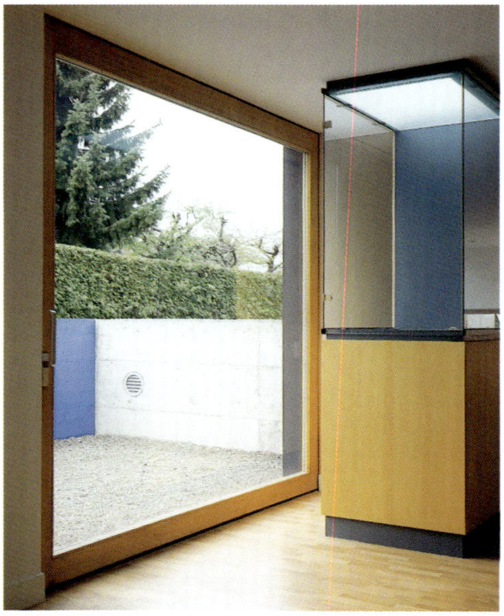

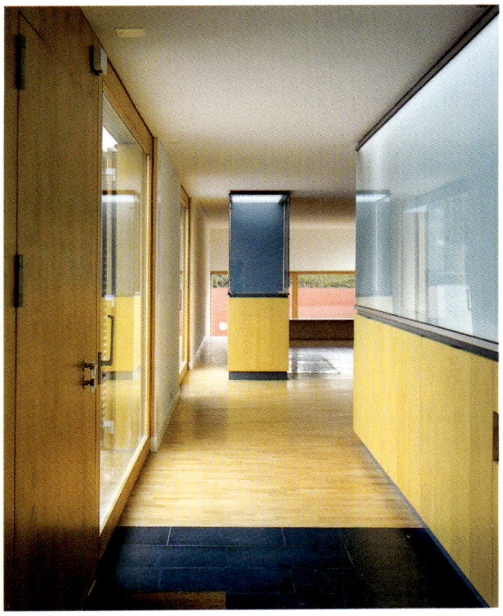

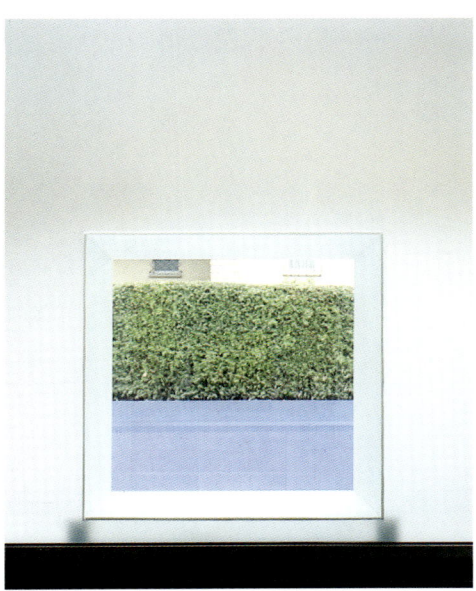

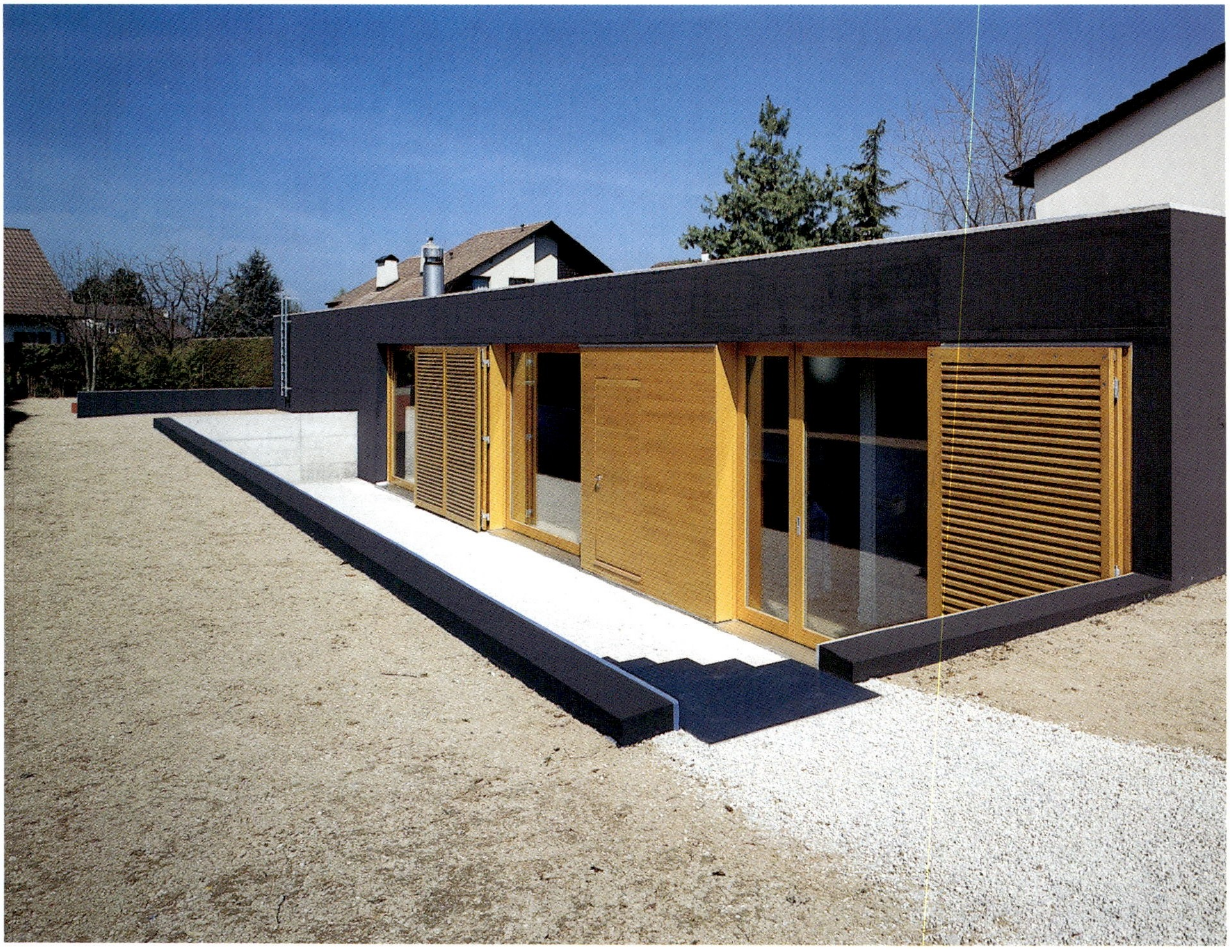

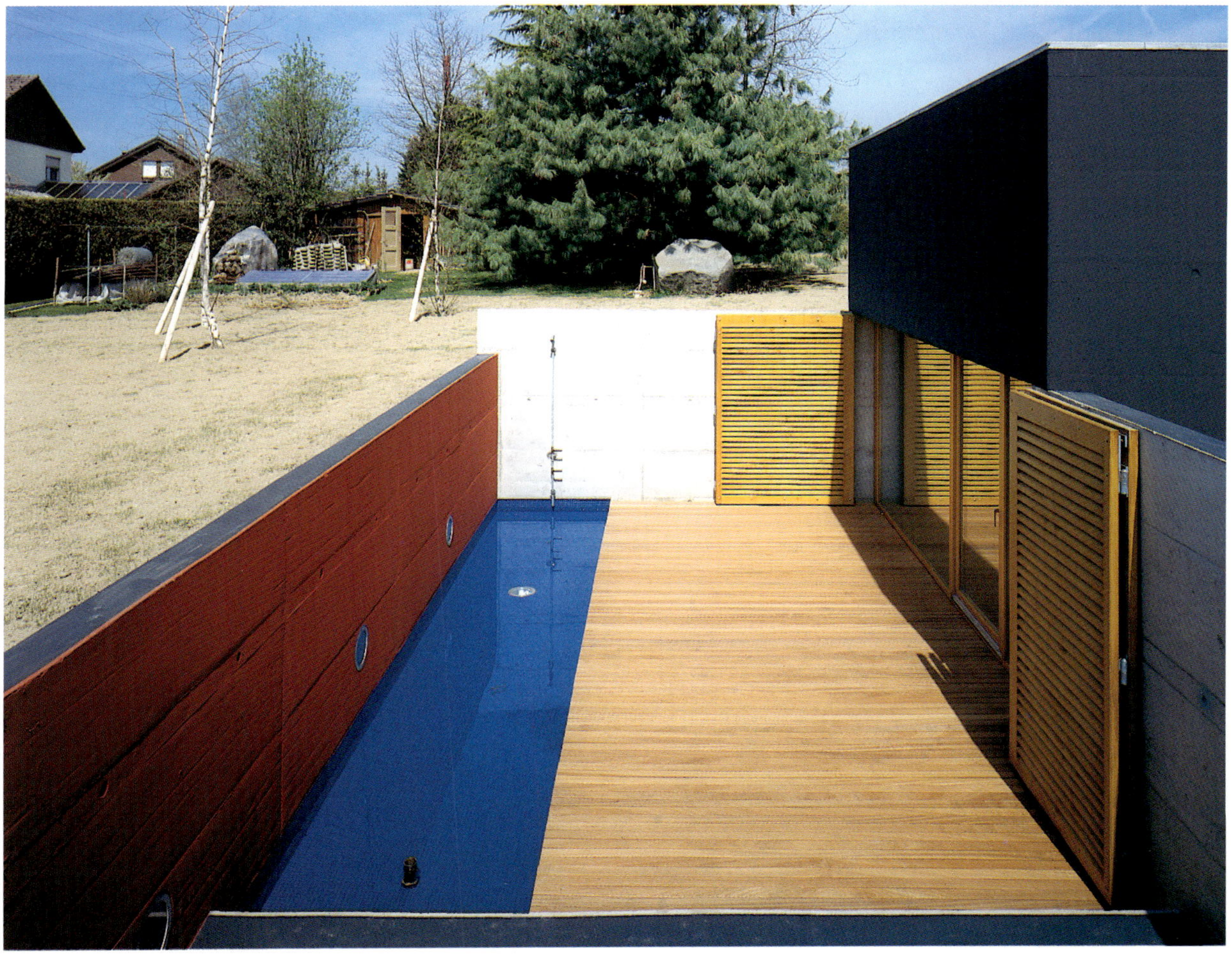

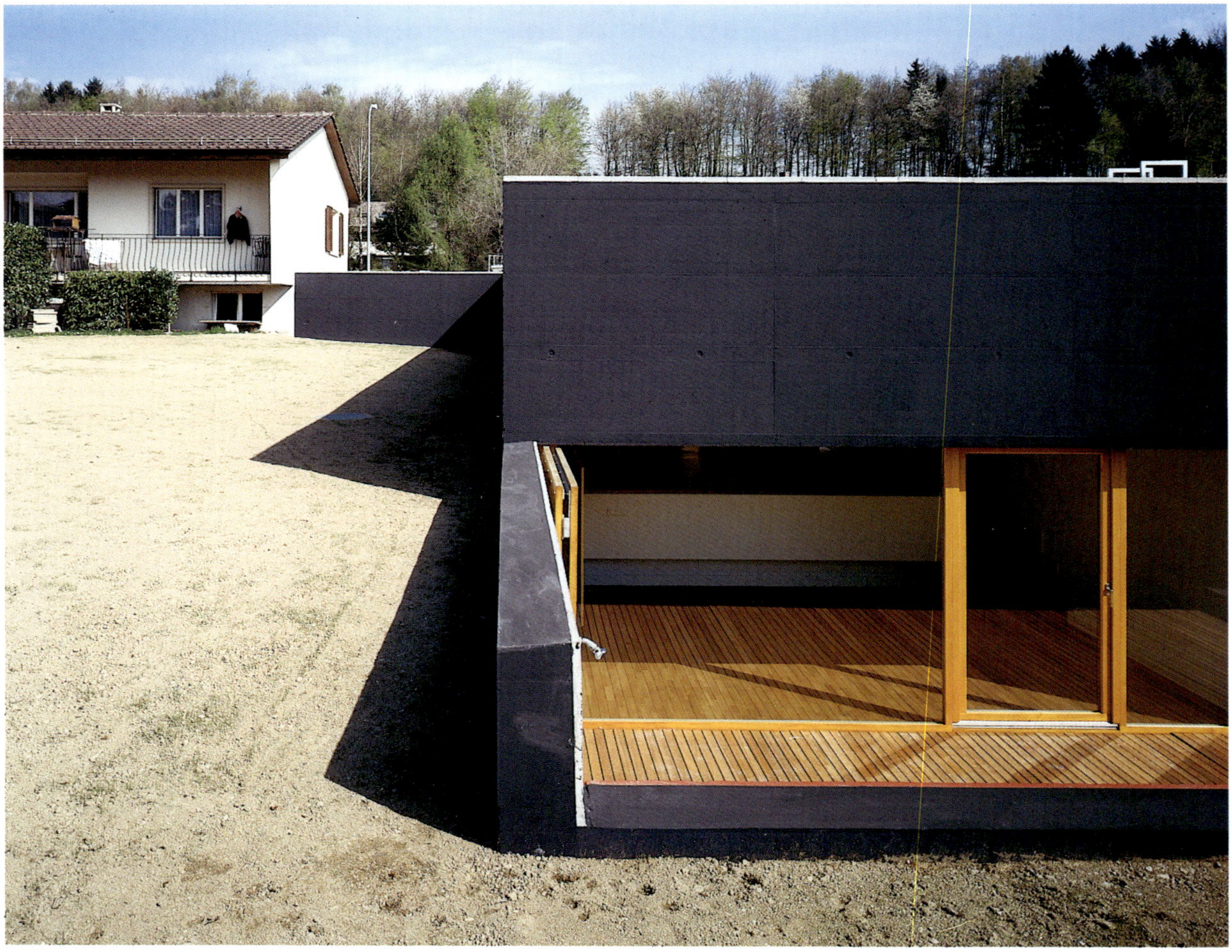

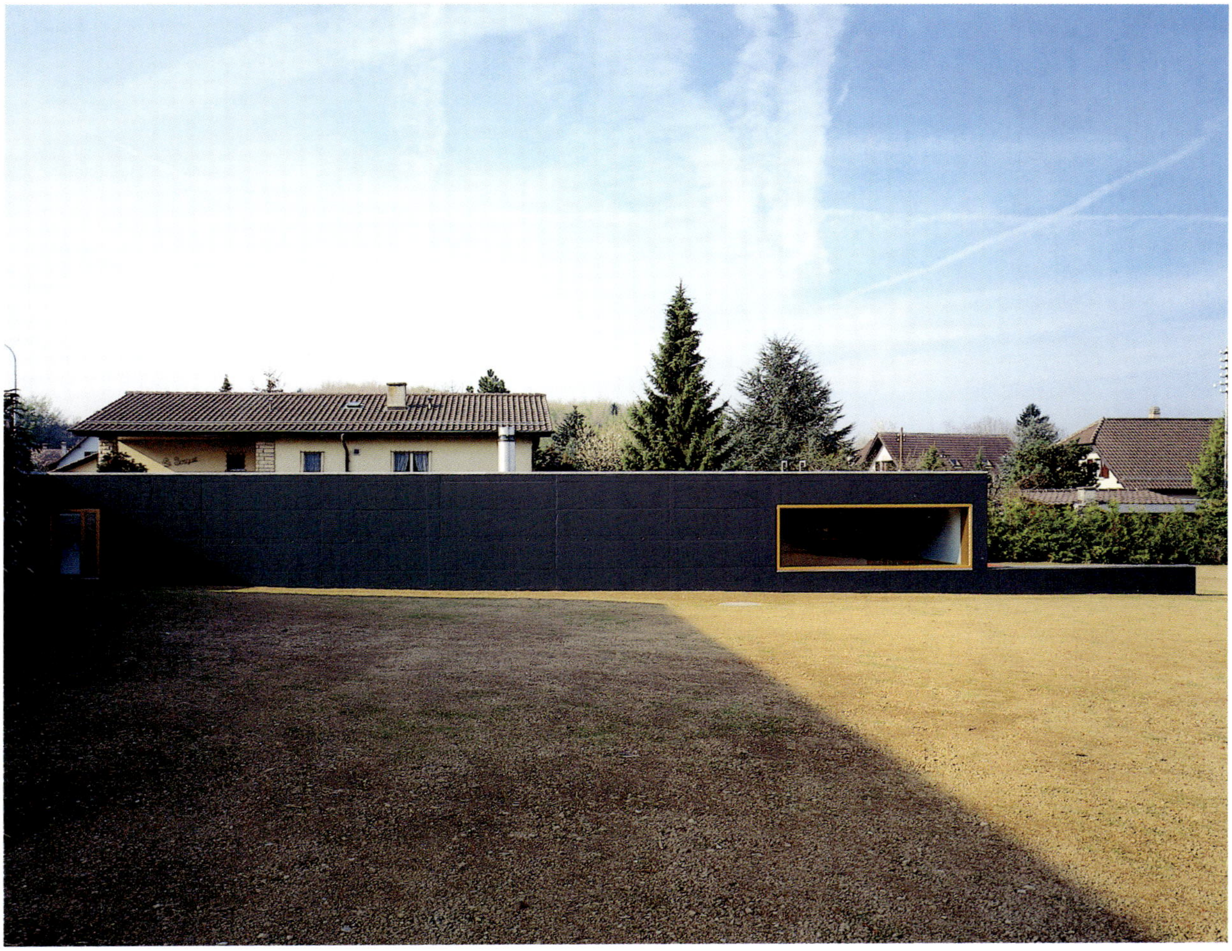

CATALOGUE OF PROJECTS AND BUILT WORKS

This catalogue is an extract of the principal projects and built works from the period 1986 to 1996. A short text outlines the main focus of each project, followed by a list of publications and keys to selected illustrations. Each of the plans and photographs are by the authors, with the exception of those kindly provided by Sergio Cavero (SC), Alain Grandchamp (AG), Gérald Friedli (GF), Philippe Pache (PP) and Simon Lamunière (SL), to whom we would like here to express our thanks for their help.

WERKVERZEICHNIS

Dieses Verzeichnis ist eine ausgewählte Zusammenstellung der Entwürfe und Realisierungen von 1986 bis 1996. Eine Kurzbeschreibung faßt die wichtigsten Merkmale des jeweiligen Projektes zusammen; daran anschließend folgen Literaturangaben und Bildlegenden. Die Pläne und Fotografien sind von den Autoren, sofern als Fotografen nicht ausdrücklich Sergio Cavero (SC), Alain Grandchamp (AG), Gérald Friedli (GF), Philippe Pache (PP) oder Simon Lamunière (SL) erwähnt sind, denen an dieser Stelle für ihre Mitarbeit gedankt sei.

**Patrick Devanthéry and
Inès Lamunière**

1954 Born in Sion and Geneva
1980 Diploma in architecture, EPFL
(Prof. Joseph Rykwert, Jacques Gubler, Paolo Portoghesi)
1981–1983 Members of the Swiss Institute of Rome – FNRS grant
1983 Association Patrick Devanthéry & Inès Lamunière, Architects, in Geneva and Lausanne
1983–88 Teaching in Geneva (P.D.) and Zurich (I.L.)
Since 1989 Editors of the journal *Faces – Journal d'architectures de l'Université de Genève*
1991–93 Assistant professor at the EPFZ (I.L.)
Since 1993 Professor at the EPFL (I.L.)
1994 Visiting professor at the EPFZ (P.D.)
1996 Visiting professors at Harvard University

Collaborators

Principal collaborators: Isabelle Charollais and Olivier Andreotti. Collaborators:
P. Aeby, M. Barth, L. Bionda (1987–90), M. Ducrey (1993–96), F. de Marignac, L. Matthey, Ph. Meylan (1989–94), S. Schmidt (1990–1993), B. Stanton, A. Wagnières. Office staff: Y. Gattegno, I. Ketterer and C. Pahud (1986–91). Student collaborators (1986–96): A. Berger, S. Chessex, Y. Delgado, S. Jordan, H. Lacroix. V. Lipp, D. Meier, M.-L. Naef, E. Ogay, S. Pétremand, C. Rotzetter, A. Schwartz and M. Voechting.

**Patrick Devanthéry und
Inès Lamunière**

1954 geboren in Sitten bzw. Genf
1980 Diplomabschlüsse an der Eidgenössischen Technischen Hochschule Lausanne (Joseph Rykwert, Jacques Gubler, Paolo Portoghesi)
1981–1983 Mitarbeiter des Schweizer Instituts von Rom, Stipendium des Schweizerischen Nationalfonds
1983 Gründung der Association Patrick Devanthéry & Inès Lamunière, Architekten in Genf und Lausanne
1983–1988 Lehraufträge in Genf (P.D.) und Zürich (I.L.)
seit 1989 Redakteure der Zeitschrift *Faces – Journal d'architectures de l'Université de Genève*
1991–1993 Assistenzprofessur an der ETH Zürich (I.L.)
seit 1993 ordentliche Professur an der EPFL (I.L.)
1994 Gastprofessur an der ETH Zürich (P.D.)
1996 Gastprofessuren an der Harvard University

Mitarbeiterinnen und Mitarbeiter

Hauptmitarbeitende: Isabelle Charollais und Olivier Andreotti. Weitere Mitarbeitende:
P. Aeby, M. Barth, L. Bionda (1987–90), M. Ducrey (1993–96), F. de Marignac, L. Matthey, Ph. Meylan (1989–94), S. Schmidt (1990–93), B. Stanton, A. Wagnières. Sekretariat: Y. Gattegno, I. Ketterer und C. Pahud (1986–91). Praktikanten (1986–96): A. Berger, S. Chessex, Y. Delgado, S. Jordan, H. Lacroix, V. Lipp, D. Meier, M.-L. Naef, E. Ogay, S. Pétremand, C. Rotzetter, A. Schwartz und M. Voechting.

CATALOGUE / WERKVERZEICHNIS

1.1

1.2

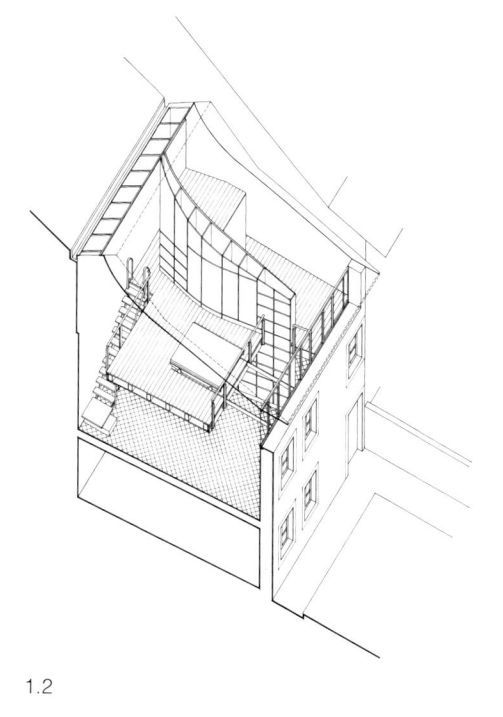

1. Conversion and upward extension in a historic village / Wohnungsumwandlung und -aufstockung in einem historischen Stadtkern

Built: 1985–86, Rue Davel 28, Cully, VD

A small interior, fifty square meters in area, on two levels, is enclosed by three walls and one facade. The convex shape of the central element containing the service elements of the program enlarges the perception of the spaces it divides. The raised roof detaches itself from the walls, and the contour of the suspended ceiling accentuates the incoming light.

/ Ein kleiner Innenraum von 50 m², auf zwei Etagen, wird von drei Mauern und einer Fassade umfasst. Die konvexe Form des zentral eingebauten Gliederungselements, das die Servicräume aufnimmt, läßt die beiden Raumhälften größer erscheinen. Die erhöht gesetzte Dachkonstruktion, deren Lichtwirkung durch die zum Durchhang gebogene Zwischendecke betont wird, hebt sich von den Mauern ab.

Architecture suisse no 80, 1987
«*Positionen*», Ed. Boga, Zurich, 1988
L'Hebdo no. 31, Lausanne, August 1989
Ideales Heim nos. 1/7/8, Zurich, 1990
Portraits d'architecture vaudoise, Lausanne, 1989
Prize: Selected for the Vaud distinction in architecture, 1989

1.1 View of the skylight and the suspended ceiling (AG)
1.2 Axonometric projection

2. New hospital of Sierre / Neues Krankenhaus von Siders

Competition, 2nd prize, 1986, Sierre, VS

In association with Ph. & R. Renaud and B. Marchand

A long inward-curving building reorients the hospital complex towards the older, turn-of-the-century building.

/ Ein langes, gekrümmtes Gebäude wird an den Anfang Jahrhundert entstandenen Altbau des Spitals angegliedert.

Werk, Bauen und Wohnen no. 3, 1987

3. A public services building (post office, public works department, fire department) and five apartments / Gebäude für Betriebe (Post, Straßenbauamt, Feuerwehr) und fünf Wohnungen

Competition, 1st prize, 1986
Built: 1988–90, Le Sancy, Commune de Villars-Ste-Croix, VD
Collaborator: Lionel Bionda

On a site on the edge of the village, the building reunites the numerous and disparate programs in a whole which expresses its individual parts. The painted wood surfaces of the apartments, the standardised metal doors of the works department and the concrete frame of the post office are united by the brick of the parallelepiped.

/ Das auf einem Grundstück am Rande des Dorfes gelegene Gebäude versammelt zahlreiche und disparate Elemente von Bauprogramm und Ort zu einem Ganzen, das seine Zusammensetzung zu erkennen gibt. Die gestrichene Holzaußenfläche des Wohnbereichs, die Metalltüren in Standardausführung des Straßenbauamts und der Betonrahmen der Post werden zusammengefaßt durch das Ziegelsteinmauerwerk des Baukubus.

«*Positionen*», Ed. Boog, Zurich, 1988
Faces no. 16, Geneva, Summer 1990
Architecture suisse, no. 97, June 1991
Portraits d'architecture vaudoise, Lausanne, 1992
Prize: Special mention for the Vaud distinction in architecture, 1992

3.1 Typical section
3.2 View of the east facade: services (PP)

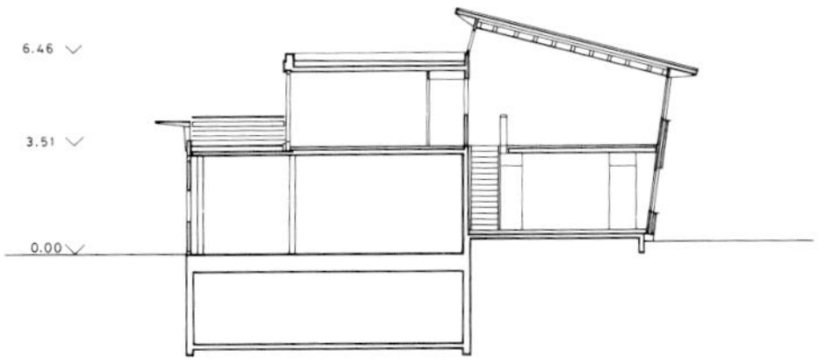

3.3 View of the west facade: apartments (PP)
3.4 View of the north facade: post office (PP)

4. Exhibition *Le Corbusier in Geneva, 1922–1932* / Realisierung der Ausstellung «*Le Corbusier in Genf, 1922–1932*»

May 1987, 'Clarté', Geneva (catalogue)

Consultants for the exhibition, *L'aventure Le Corbusier,* Centre Georges Pompidou, Paris, November 1987 (catalogue).

/ Danach Berater für die Ausstellung «*L'aventure Le Corbusier*», Centre Georges Pompidou, Paris, November 1987 (Katalog).

5. Housing in the vineyards / Wohnsiedlung in den Weinbergen

Competition, 2nd prize, 1987, Aubonne, VD

A typology of two superimposed duplexes organises the three buildings along the slope of the vineyards.

/ Drei am Hang eines Weinbergs gelegene Gebäude werden typologisch organisiert durch je zwei sich überlagernde Duplex-Wohnungen.

Habitation no. 11, 1987

6. Village community hall / Dörfliches Gemeindezentrum

Competition, special mention, 1988, Tannay, VD

A single ramp, masked by wooden lattice work, reorganises the spaces of the barn and the existing brick buildings, enabling this fragment of village heritage to be preserved.

3.1

3.2

3.3

3.4

/ Durch eine einzige, mit einem Holzgeländer versehene Rampe reorganisieren sich die Räume der Scheune und existierenden Mauerwerksbauten und ermöglichen damit die Erhaltung dieses Stücks dörflichen Erbes.

7. Four tunnel portals for the Transjurane highway / Vier Tunnelpforten für die Transjura-Autobahn

Competition, 1988, Delémont, JU

Each portal is made of stone blocks extracted from the geological strata of the Jura mountains. Placed one on top of the other, they express in appropriate geometrical figures, the archaic laws of gravity and compression. The project forms the landscape of an 'interior' nature which became through its construction, 'exterior'.

/ Die Pforten sind aus Gesteinsblöcken errichtet, die dem Tafeljura entstammen. Diese sind zu schlichten geometrischen Figuren aufeinandergesetzt, die von den uralten Gesetzen der Schwerkraft und Kompression geprägt sind. In diesem Projekt wird die Natur das «Erd-Innere» durch den baulichen Eingriff nach aussen gekehrt.

Faces no. 11, Spring 1989

7.1 Model of the Gripons portal

8. Exhibition: 'Positionen': Atelier Cube, Devanthéry & Lamunière and Mestelan & Gachet / Ausstellung: «Positionen»: Atelier Cube, Devanthéry & Lamunière und Mestelan & Gachet

September 1988, Architekturforum Zurich (catalogue)

9. Schwarz-Park residential housing for 300 apartments / Wohnviertel mit 300 Wohnungen im Schwarz-Park

Competition, 1st prize, 1988
Project, 1988–91, Gellertstrasse, Basel
A vote by the population of the canton on 6.12.1991 allowed for the redesignation of the area from a building zone into a green zone.
Collaborators: Isabelle Charollais and Sébastien Schmidt

Three nine-storey buildings insert into the space between the top of the site and the bottom, or three «altimeters» whose staggered, curving volumes give a sense of depth to the park; three identical buildings contrasting with the variety of the countryside. From the large terraces placed in the park at 12 metres above the level of the meadow, occurs the distribution towards the upper portion, of the flats, and towards the lower portion, of the duplexes.

/ Drei neungeschossige Gebäude schreiben sich auf unterschiedlicher Höhe in das abfallende Gelände ein. Die versetzten Krümmungen ihrer Baukörper geben dem Park eine Tiefendimension. Drei gleiche Gebäudeeinheiten werden der Vielfalt des Parks gegenübergestellt. Von den großen Terrassen aus, die sich 12 m über dem Erdboden befinden, verteilen sich nach oben die eingeschossigen Appartements, nach unten die Duplex-Wohnungen.

Journal de Genève, 16–17 April 1988
Hochparterre, November 1988, pp. 18–19
'Positionen' Ed. Boga, Zurich, 1988
Aktuelle Wettbewerbs Scene no. 3-4, 1988
Werk, Bauen und Wohnen no. 12, Zurich, December 1989
Baumeister no. 1, Munich, January 1990

9.1 Plan of typical upper-floor appartments
9.2 Study model for one bay of the building

9.1

9.2   10.1   10.2

10. Apartment building for students, Centre Universitaire Protestant 2 / Wohnheim für Studierende, Centre Universitaire Protestant 2

Project, 1988, built: 1991–93; Boulevard-de-la-Tour 1, Geneva
Collaborator: Isabelle Charollais

The project is a response to the complex character of the site: its L-shaped volume aligns itself with the flat surfaces of the rue du Petit-Salève facade, returns onto the elevated garden of the rue Micheli-du-Crest, and confronts the horizontal lines of a curving facade and the verticals of the attic frames on Boulevard-de-la-Tour. A typology of apartments with double entrances preserves the intimacy of the identical student rooms; the kitchen-living areas are more open, reflecting the geometries of the site.

10.3

10.4

/ Das Gebäude trägt dem komplexen Charakter der Gegend Rechnung, in die es sich einbindet: Mit seinem L-förmigen Baukörper paßt es sich der glatten Fassadenfront der Rue du Petit-Salève an und umgreift an der Rue Micheli-du-Crest den Terrassengarten. Richtung Boulevard-de-la-Tour treffen die Horizontalität des gekrümmten Fassadenschirms und die Vertikalität der Attika-Rahmen aufeinander. Die Appartements besitzen jeweils zwei Eingänge, wodurch die Intimität der Studentenzimmer gewahrt bleibt. Diese sind als gleichförmige Zellen angelegt. Die Wohn-Küchen-Bereiche gestalten sich freier und passen sich den Geometrien des jeweiligen Standortes an.

Techniques et Architecture, Paris, no. 380, 1988
'Positionen', Ed. Boga, 1988
Baumeister no. 1, Munich, January 1990
Archithese no. 4, July-August 1993
Construction no.11, 15. 9. 93
Architecture suisse no. 111, March 1994
Neue Zürcher Zeitung, p. 67, 6 May 1994
Journal de l'immobilier, Geneva, no. 21, 11 May 1994
Faces no. 32, Summer 1994
AMC-Le Moniteur no. 58, February 1995
L'éveil culturel, September 1995
Habitation, no. 5, 1995
Le nouveau quotidien, 26 October 1995
Matière et fabrique, DA Information, no. 165, EPFL, Lausanne, 1995

10.1 View of the northern corner of the Boulevard-de-la-Tour (AG)
10.2 View of the courtyard overlooking Micheli-du-Crest (AG)
10.3 View of the southern corner of the Boulevard-de-la-Tour (AG)
10.4 View of the facade overlooking Petit-Salève (AG)

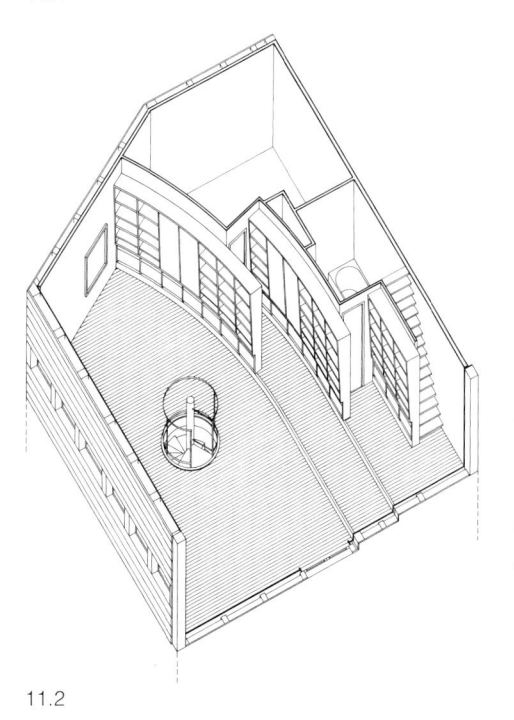

11. Private library in an existing house / Ausbau eines Dachbodens zur Privatbibliothek

Built: 1989, Chemin des Limites 10, Bellevue, GE

Conversion of the attic space in a barn into a library for living and working. Three groups of convex, self-supporting shelves are staggered to reinforce the effect of wings or decor. Two of the four walls were panelled in dark wood like the library shelves. In one wall, a continuous window has been inserted at the level of a seated person; its construction between the existing timbering accentuates the sequential image of the panorama.

/ Der Dachboden einer Scheune wurde zum Bibliotheks-, Wohn- und Arbeitsraum ausgebaut. Drei gekrümmte und freitragende Regalelemente stehen losgelöst im Raum, so daß sich der Eindruck von Kulisse oder Dekor verstärkt. Zwei der vier Wände wurden mit dunklem Holz verkleidet, wie es sich häufig in Bibliotheken findet. In eine davon ist auf Kopfhöhe eines Sitzenden ein bandartiges Fenster eingefügt. Dadurch, daß es zwischen die bereits vorhandenen Fachwerkbalken gesetzt ist, wird das Panorama in einzelne Sequenzen zerstückelt.

Architecture suisse, no. 94, Lausanne, 1990
Journal de Genève, 9.8.1990
Rivista Tecnica no. 3, Lugano, 1991
Faces no. 23, Spring 1992
Archithese no. 5, September 1992
Innenarchitektur in der Schweiz 1942–1992, Niggli Verlag, 1993

11.1 View of the library partition walls (AG)
11.2 Axonometric projection

12.1

12.2

12.3

12. Exhibition: *Saffa 1928, 1958 und heute? Ein Projekt von Inès Lamunière, Flora Ruchat and Beate Schnitter* / Ausstellung: *Saffa 1928, 1958 und heute? Ein Projekt von Inès Lamunière, Flora Ruchat und Beate Schnitter*

April–June 1989, Architekturmuseum, Basel

The project for a SAFFA exhibition entered directly into history through the doors of the museum... Oriented to the message that 'woman' no longer exists; that there are many women, all kinds of women, every woman; the exhibition is oriented to the manifestations of this state (word, text, gestures, femininity).

/ Das Projekt einer SAFFA (Schweizerische Ausstellung für Frauenarbeit) wurde für einmal paradoxerweise direkt als Museumsausstellung konzipiert. Orientiert an dem Leitgedanken, daß «die» Frau nicht mehr existiert, sondern es Frauen gibt, viele und jede einzeln, versucht die Ausstellung den vielfältigen Weisen, in denen Frauen sich manifestieren, gerecht zu werden (Wort, Schrift, Geste, «Weiblichkeit»).

12.1 Installation on the first floor: women with a thousand facets
12.2 Installation on the second floor: words of women
12.3 Installation on the third floor: women in movement

13. New cantonal hospital / Neues Kantonsspital

Competition, 7th prize, 1989, Hôpital de Pourtalès, Neuchâtel
In association with P. & R. Renaud and B. Marchand

Habitation no. 5, 1989
Ingénieurs et architectes suisses no. 26, 1989

14. School centre / Schulzentrum

Competition, 3rd prize, 1989, Orsière, VS

Facing the rocky outline of the Alps, this project signifies the artistry of the engineer; a large reinforced concrete girder is inhabited by classes and a gymnasium.

/ Dem Felsmassiv der Alpen hält der Entwurf die Kunst der Ingenieurstechnik entgegen: Schulzimmer und Sporthalle sind in einer großen, balkenartigen Eisenbetonstruktur untergebracht.

15. A market square / Marktplatz

Competition, 2nd prize, 1989, Bex, VD

At the junction between the mountain and the plain, the project for the market square uses the symbolism of the space, banal and empty, little by little marked by the saline concretions of the emergence of a salt water spring from the granite ground.

/ Der Entwurf für einen Platz, Ort der Begegnung zwischen Berg- und Talwelt, spielt mit dem Zeichenhaften der alltäglichen und gewöhnlichen Leere, wo sich im Laufe der Zeit die Spuren der salzhaltigen Ablagerungen einer direkt dem Granitboden entspringenden Quelle abzeichnen werden.

Aktuelle Wettbewerbs Scene no. 6, 1989
Architektur & Wettbewerbe no. 144, 1990

17.1

17.2

16. A primary school and a leisure centre / Grundschule und Freizeitzentrum

Competition, 1st prize, 1989, built: 1992–95;
Route de Colovrex, Grand-Saconnex, GE
Collaborator: Olivier Andreotti

Ingénieurs et Architectes suisses no. 4, 1990
Faces no. 40, Autumn 1996
Matière et fabrique, DA Information, no. 165, EPFL, Lausanne, 1995

17. Renovation of the swimming complex at Bellerive-Plage / Restaurierung der Bäder von Bellerive-Plage

Restoration: 1990–93; originally built by Marc Piccard (1937), Avenue de Rhodanie, Ouchy, Lausanne
Collaborator: Philippe Meylan

Restoring an existing reinforced concrete building realised during a time when an abundant workforce and low-cost materials were available, enabled techniques and methods appropriate to the 'poor' concrete around a complex restoration project. It allowed also through meticulous observation, the habilitation and preservation of one of the most ingenious functionalities; where form, distribution and function form a pertinent whole.

/ Ein Gebäude aus Stahlbeton restaurieren, das in einer Wirtschaftsperiode des Überflusses an Arbeitskräften und gleichzeitigen Booms von Sparmaterialien errichtet wurde, hieß, im Rahmen eines komplexen Reparaturvorhabens Techniken und Konzepte entwickeln, die einem «ärmlichen» Beton gerecht würden. Gleichzeitig ging es darum, eine der feinstdurchdachten Funktionalarchitekturen, bei der Form, Gliederung und Funktion eine vollkommene Einheit bilden, durch minuziöse Analyse zu erfassen, um Instandsetzung und Erhalt zu ermöglichen.

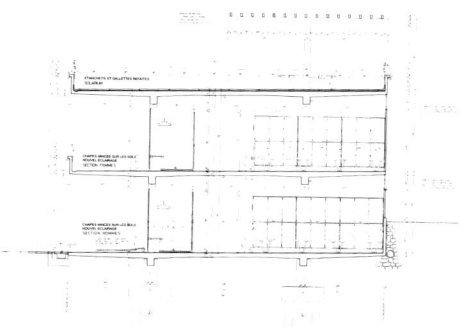

17.3

Rassegna no. 49, March 1992
Construction no. 11, 15.09.93
Docomomo, 10 November 1993
Faces no. 29, Autumn 1993
Tema no. 1, 1994
Werk Bauen und Wohnen no. 3, March 1994
Area no. 18, June 1994
Matière et fabrique, DA Information no 165, EPFL, Lausanne, 1995
Les Bains de Bellerive, J. Gubler et al., Ed. Payot, Lausanne, 1996
Prize: Vaud distinction in architecture, 1996

17.1 The solarium
17.2 The rotunda
17.3 Typical section through the changing cabins

18. A music room in an existing private house / Privates Musikzimmer in einem bestehenden Wohnhaus

Built: 1990; Chemin des Limites 8, Bellevue, GE
Collaborator: Lionel Bionda

In a room of reinforced concrete, carved out, the project traces the depth of the level of the ground by a fragile facing in birch wood; the trapezoid geometry accentuates the detachment between the domestic space for listening and that of its receptacle.

/ Ein Zimmer im Halbkeller aus Stahlbeton konstruiert. Bis hin zur Linie der Erdoberfläche wurde es mit einer hellen Verkleidung aus Birkenholz versehen. Die trapezförmige Geometrie betont die Trennung von Wohn- und Zuhörerraum und jenem Raum, wo die Musik entsteht.

Rivista Tecnica no. 3, Lugano June 1991

18.1 Panels (SL)

18.1

20.1

19. A room in a garden / Zimmer zum Garten

Built: 1990; Rue des Moraines 8, Carouge, GE
Collaborator: Isabelle Charollais

Extension of an existing house with a painted wooden container, raised above the garden. The convex wall and the large window unify the interior and project it towards the outside.

/ Wohnhauserweiterung in Form eines gestrichenen Holz-Containers, der erhöht über dem Garten liegt. Die gekrümmte Wand und das große Fenster bündeln den Innenraum, um ihn dann trichterförmig nach aussen zu projizieren.

Journal de Genève, 31.8.1991
Faces no. 23, Spring 1992
AMC – Le Moniteur, nos. 32–33, June–July 1992
Archithese no. 5, September 1995
Séquences Bois no. 6, September 1995

19.1 Detail of the space of the window (SL)
19.2 The large window overlooking the garden (SL)

20. A school of agriculture / Landwirtschaftsschule

Competition, 2nd prize, 1990, Grange-Verney, VD

The traces of ancient enclosures of agricultural fiefs organises the plan of the workshops and the classrooms. Conceived according to the structural principles of industrial building, implicit in the large structural spans they divert the traditional and archaic materials of the place: stone and wood.

/ Die Anordnung der Unterrichts- und Werkräume orientiert sich an dem, was von den früheren Grenzen des landwirtschaftlichen Guts an Spuren geblieben ist. Das Konstruktionsprinzip mit den im Industriebereich üblichen großen Spannweiten, verfremdet die

traditionellen, archaischen Materialien der Gegend – Stein und Holz.

Habitation no. 7/8, 1990

20.1 Perspective view of the workshops

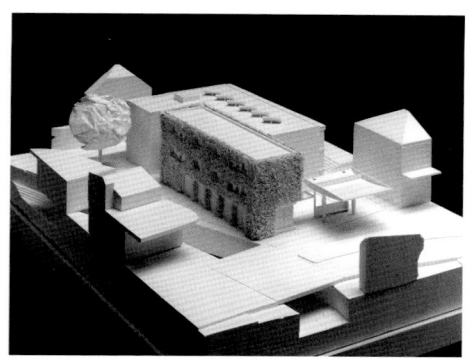

21. Crassier customs building / Zollhaus von Crassier

Commission for a preliminary study, 1990, Crassier, VD

A rectangular, masonry volume, placed at the border like a boundary stone, a simple landmark, it is covered with a trelliswork which will in time allow various ivies and green vines to reclaim it.

/ Ein rechteckiger Mauerwerksbau, auf die Grenze gesetzt wie ein Markstein, als einfacher Orientierungspunkt, ist mit einem Gitter ummantelt, das bald von Efeu und wilden Reben umrankt sein wird.

Habitation no. 9, 1990

21.1 Model (GF)

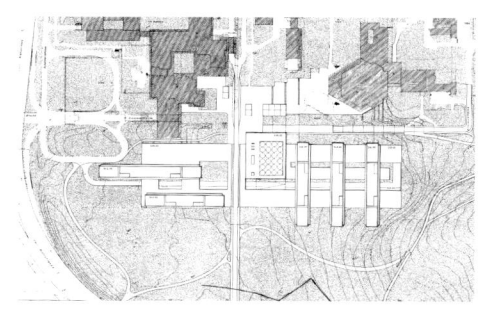

22. Extension for the ETH Zürich / Erweiterung der ETH Zürich

Competition, 1990, Hönggerberg, ZH

A large slab with patios receives the laboratories and studios. The classroom buildings emerge above it as solitary objects.

/ Ein ausgedehnter Flachbau, durchsetzt mit Innenhöfen, nimmt Laboratorien und Werkstätten auf. Über ihm ragen die Unterrichtstrakte als Solitärbauten auf.

22.1 Site plan

19.1

19.2

21.1

22.1

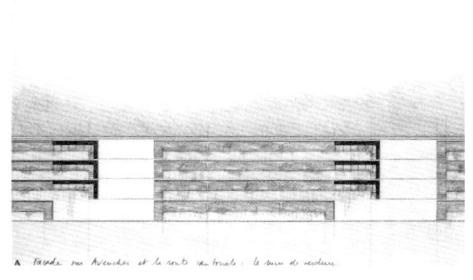

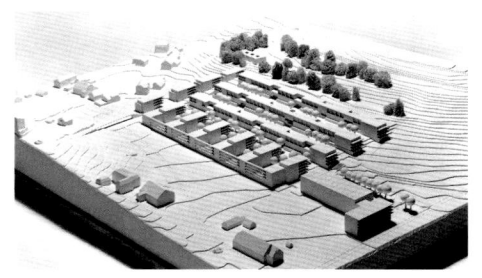

23. New facades for a thermal establishment / Neue Fassaden für ein Thermalbad

Built: 1991–92; Saillon, VS
Collaborator: Olivier Andreotti

In follow-up to an analysis which revealed serious damage due to an ill-conceived physical design of the building, the project installs new facades, or large spans of glass, placed at the exterior of the existing structures.

/ Nachdem sich in einem Gutachten schwere, auf eine physikalische Fehlkonzeption des Gebäudes zurückzuführende Schäden herausgestellt hatten, wurden den vorhandenen Strukturen neue Fassaden mit großen Glasplatten vorgeblendet.

23.1 View of the interior (SC)
23.2 The new panels on the outside (SC)

24. Restoration of the Planches bridge / Restaurierung der Brücke Pont des Planches

Project: 1991–92; original work by Melan (1912), Le Sepey, VD
Collaborator: Olivier Andreotti

Matière et fabrique, DA Information, no. 165, EPFL, Lausanne, 1995

25. Housing quarter with 300 apartments / Wohnviertel mit 300 Wohnungen

Competition: 1991, 1st prize; preliminary study: 1991–92; Sur Fourches, Avenches, VD

On a hill facing Avenches, the project builds the sector below the altitude mark of the buildings of the town, leaving the summit above as green and natural as opposed to that of Avenches which is grey and built-up. For the housing, a typology of the plain disassociates itself from a typology of the slope.

/ Auf einem Hügel gegenüber von Avenches setzt das Projekt die obere Baulinie dort fest, wo die Bebauung auf dem Hügel von Avenches erst anfängt. Damit bleibt die Hügelkuppe des Projekts ebenso grün und natürlich, wie die Ebene grau und zugebaut ist. Bei den Wohnbauten wird zwischen einer Typologie der Ebene und der Hanglage unterschieden.

Ingénieurs et architectes suisses no. 12, 1991

25.1 Facade overlooking the cantonal highway
25.2 Model

26. Ramp and commercial space at the Cornavin train station / Rampe und Kommerzflächen des Bahnhofs Cornavin

Built: 1991–93, Gare Cornavin, Geneva
Collaborator: Sébastien Schmidt

By means of a few minimal interventions in certain selected sectors of Cornavin, the project seeks to regain the large dimension of the spaces within a station. The large red wall of the ramp between the upper hall and the lower one is the first stage in achieving this aim.

/ Durch einige nur geringfügige Eingriffe an ausgewählten Stellen des Bahnhofbereichs, will der Entwurf die räumliche Großzügigkeit herstellen, nach der ein solcher Ort verlangt. Die große rote Wand der Rampe zwischen oberer und unterer Halle ist ein erster Schritt dazu.

26.1 Red glass panel with an 'orange-peel' texture (SC)

27.1

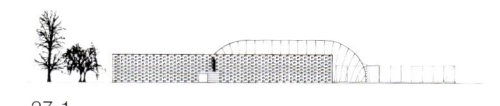

27. A contemporary arts centre / Zentrum für zeitgenössische Kunst

Commission for a feasibility study: 1991, Vidy, Lausanne
In cooperation with: André Ducret, sociologist

The project allies the regularity, proportion and solidity of the exhibition rooms with the temporality and economy of the tent structure. References are evident to the tradition of the wall and the light-diffusing qualities of an ordinary tent.

/ In diesem Entwurf verbindet sich das Reguläre, Ausgewogene und Solide der Ausstellungsräume mit dem Temporären und Wirtschaftlichen der Dachlösung. Ein Festhalten an der Tradition der Mauer und zugleich eine Anleihe ans gewöhnliche Zelt, durch dessen Tuch sich das Licht zerstreut.

Un centre d'arts plastiques contemporains à Lausanne, L. Coen and P. Keller, Lausanne, 1992
Faces no. 26, Winter 1992
L'Hebdo no. 49, December 1992
Archithese no. 5, September 1993
Matière et fabrique, DA Information, no. 165, EPFL, Lausanne, 1995

27.1 Entrance, west facade

28. Restoration of the main hall of the Bel-Air Métropole / Restaurierung des großen Saals im Bel-Air-Métropole

Project: 1992, built: 1995–97; original work by A. Laverrière (1936), Métropole, Lausanne
Collaborator: Barry Stanton. In association with: F. Jolliet and P. Lovat

Complete reorganization of the stage area, technical installations, and acoustics in the context of the restoration of this 1100 seat hall.

26.1

/ Komplette Erneuerung der Bühnentechnik, Elektroinstallationen und akustischen Vorrichtungen im Rahmen der Instandsetzung dieses 1100 Plätze fassenden Saals, der als historisches Denkmal eingestuft ist.

Werk Bauen und Wohnen no. 3, March 1994

29. A house for the Federation of Catholic Parishes / Haus für den Verbund katholischer Pfarrgemeinden

Competition, 1st prize ex-aequo, 1991; Morges, VD

A composition of volumes for lodging and for the seminary situated around a large, stripped-down central space, inspires spirituality through its quietness.

/ Die Gästezimmer und Seminarräume sind um einen großen, nackten Zentralbereich gruppiert, dessen Stille zur inneren Einkehr lädt.

29.1 Model
29.2 Plan of the buildings surrounding the large garden of broken clay

30. Renovation of the main lecture hall at the EPFL / Restaurierung der Aula der EPFL

Project: 1992; built: 1994–95; originally built by J. Tschumi (1962), Avenue de Cour 33, Lausanne
Collaborator: Mylène Ducrey

Matière et fabrique, DA Information, no. 165, EPFL, Lausanne, 1995

31. Extension for the Federal Military Department / Erweiterung des Eidgenössischen Militärdepartements

Commission for preliminary study: 1992, EMPFA, Berne

29.1

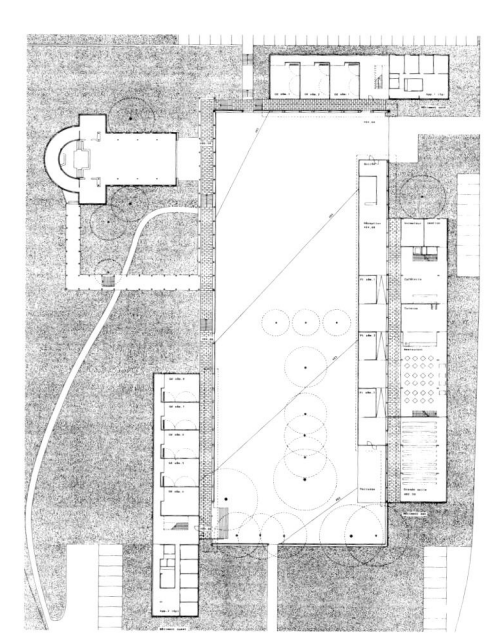

29.2

32. School at Chamblandes / Gymnasium von Chamblandes

Competition: 1992, built: 1993–96; Avenue des Desertes, Pully, VD
Collaborators: Isabelle Charollais and Michel Barth

Espace no. 18, March 1993
Archithese no. 4, July–August 1993
Matière et fabrique, DA Information, no. 165, EPFL, Lausanne, 1995

33. Renovation of a large duplex in the 'Clarté' building / Restaurierung einer großen Duplex-Wohnung im Wohnhaus «Clarté»

Built: 1993–94; originally built by Le Corbusier and Pierre Jeanneret (1932), Rue St-Laurent 2, Geneva
Collaborator: Mylène Ducrey

An implementation of the principles of a complete restoration upon the facades and interior of an exemplary apartment.

/ Anwendung der für eine Gesamtrestaurierung des Gebäudes entwickelten Verfahren auf Fassade und Innenraum eines exemplarischen Appartements.

AMC – Le Moniteur, no. 65, October 1995

34. A studio for graphic artists in a barn / Graphikeratelier in einem Scheunenbau

Built: 1993–94, Le Cannelet, Athenaz, GE
Collaborator: Patrick Aeby

A wooden container, with its own windows, roof and skylight, inserts into the barn, leaving the vast 'residual' space untouched.

/ Ein Holz-Container mit eigenen Fenstern, Dach und Oberlicht ist in die Scheune eingeschoben, und zwar so, daß große unberührte «Reste» bleiben.

35.1

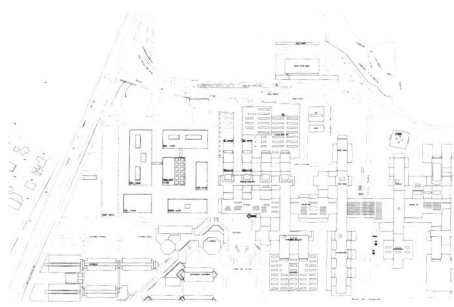

35.2

36.1

36.2

36.3

35. Extension for the EPFL / Erweiterung der EPFL

Competiton: 1993, Dorigny-Ecublens, Lausanne

On a large inclined plane which links the reception areas with the existing distribution levels, several simple, large, deep and flexible-use volumes regroup the new departments of the school, the polytechnical 'city' where streets and squares form through relations of proximity between functions.

/ Auf einer großen geneigten Fläche, die den Eingangsbereich mit der Ebene der bestehenden Erschließungen verbindet, befinden sich mehrere einfache, große und in ihrer Nutzung flexible Bauten für die neuen Fachbereiche der Hochschule. Ein polytechnisches «Städtchen», wo sich Straßen und Plätze aus dem Distanzverhältnis zwischen den einzelnen Nutzungskomplexen ergeben.

Faces no. 30, Winter 1993/1994

35.1 View of the polytechnic city
35.2 Site plan

36. Headquarters of the World Meteorology Organization / Sitz der UN Weltorganisation für Meteorologie

Competition: 1993, Avenue de la Paix, Geneva

The project is a 'block of quartz'; it marks time and weather (the facade on the Avenue de la Paix responds to the surrounding climate via photovoltaic cells) and it emerges from the depths of the supporting geology (angular, crystalline volume).

/ Das Gebäude ist wie ein Quarz: Es gibt Aufschluß über Uhrzeit und Wetterprognosen (an der Fassade Richtung Avenue de la Paix wird das Klima verschiedener Weltregionen photovoltaisch angezeigt) und scheint geologischen Tiefenschichten zu entstammen (kantiger und kristalliner Bauköper).

Archithese no. 4, July–August 1993

36.1 Model of the west side
36.2 Model of the side facing Avenue de la Paix
36.3 Avenue de la Paix facade

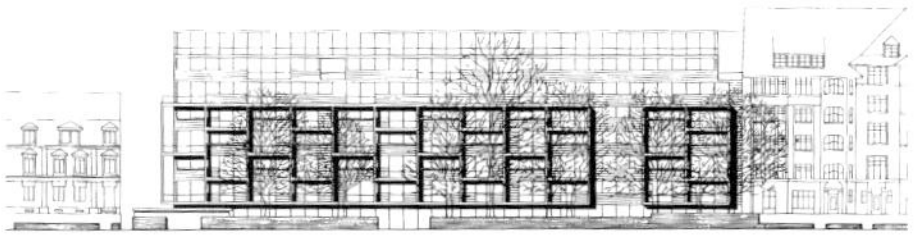

37. A housing building on the Rhine riverbank / Wohnhaus am Rheinufer

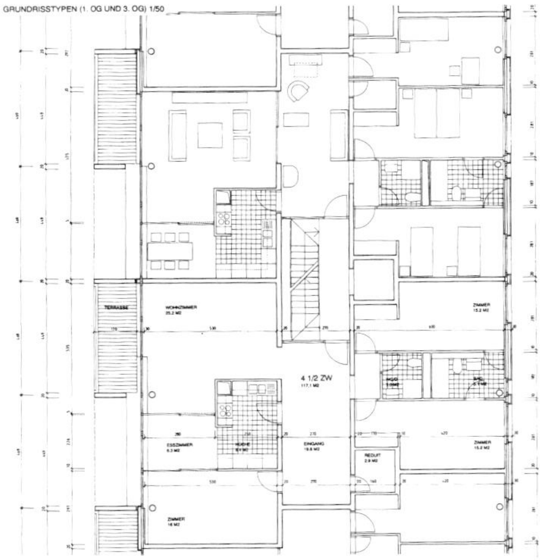

Commission for a preliminary study: 1993; Unterer Rheinweg, Basel

To evacuate the building core of its habitual service elements and propose a large hall – a communal room, a shaded alternative to the transparence of the open facades facing the Rhine in the west.

/ Das Herz der Wohnung wird befreit von den üblichen Serviceräumen zugunsten einer großzügigen Halle, die als Gemeinschaftsraum funktioniert und eine schattige Alternative zur lichtdurchfluteten, nach Westen orientierten Rheinfassade bildet.

Archithese no. 4, July–August 1993

37.1 Facade facing the Rhine
37.2 Typical floor plan for one bay of apartments

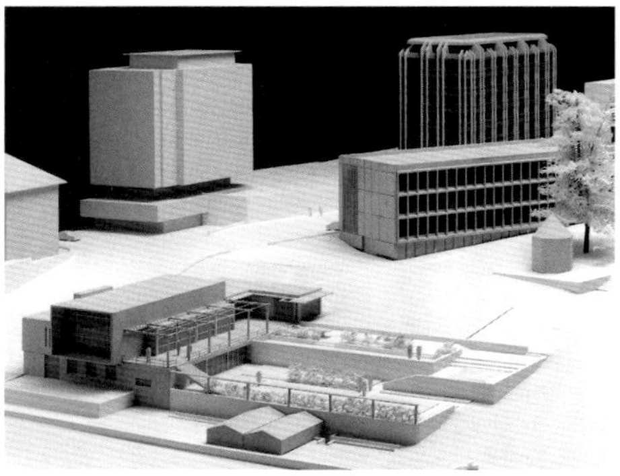

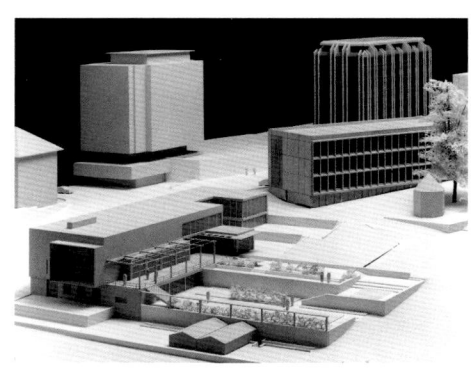

38. Staff dining hall at the Vaudoise insurance company building / Aufenthaltsraum für das Personal der Vaudoise Versicherungsgesellschaft

Restoration: 1994–95, originally built by J. Tschumi (1954)
Extension built: 1996– , Avenue des Bains, Lausanne
Collaborator: Mylène Ducrey

A close observation of the qualities of the building and its garden drove the project towards a very careful restoration of the existing structure and the proposal for an upward extension. The architecture of the extension does not contrast but creates a continuity with the original elements (concrete on concrete, no joints).

/ Nach genauer Analyse der Eigenschaften
von Gebäude und Garten ging die
Entscheidung dahin, das Vorhandene sorfältig
zu restaurieren und durch Aufstockung zu
erweitern. Die Aufstockung ist nicht auf Kontrast
angelegt, sondern auf Kontinuität (Beton auf
Beton, ohne sichtbare Fugen).

38.1 Model of existing situation (GF)
38.2 Model with upward extension (GF)

39. Renovation of 'Le Paris' cinema / Restaurierung des Kinos «Le Paris»

Project: 1994–95, built: 1996; originally built by M.-J. Saugey (1954), Avenue du Mail, Geneva
Collaborators: Patrick Aeby and Alexandre Wagnière

40. An interior for the Mayor / Interieur für eine Bürgermeisterin

Built: 1994, Chemin du Village 33, Chailly, Lausanne
Collaborator: Philippe Meylan

41. Extension of a house in a garden / Hauserweiterung zum Garten hin

Built: 1994–95; Route Suisse 15, Coppet, VD
Collaborators: Laurent Matthey and Philippe Meylan

A slab, a window pane and a 'chimney as furniture-piece' build in the garden an interior open to the lake.

/ Eine Fußbodenplatte, eine Glaswand und
ein «Kaminmöbel» lassen einen Innenraum
im auf den See geöffneten Garten entstehen.

41.1 View of the trees and the lake above the 'chimney as furniture-piece'
41.2 View of the extension in the garden

41.1

41.2

42. Villa Gringet / Villa Gringet

Project: 1994, built: 1995–95, Chemin de Faulieu, Cugy, VD
Collaborator: Patrick Aeby

43. Transformation of a rural house / Umwandlung eines ländlichen Wohnhauses

Built: 1994–95, La Grangette, Burdignin, Haute-Savoie
Collaborator: Patrick Aeby

Four huge square windows open to the four cardinal points, and modify the geometry of the domestic spaces.

/ Vier quadratische und extrem große Fenster blicken in die vier Himmelsrichtungen und lassen die Geometrie der Wohnräume verändert erscheinen.

43.1 View of one of the oblique partition walls in the trapezoid shaped living room
43.2 Plan

43.1

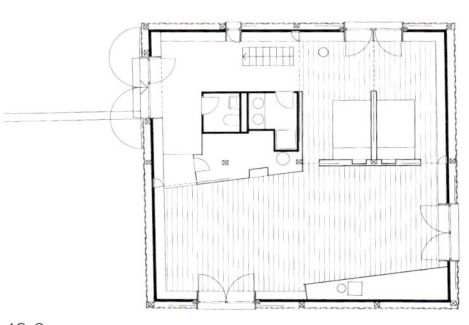

43.2

44. National exhibition 2001 / Landesausstellung 2001

Project for the Geneva proposal: 1994–95, Plaine de l'Aire, Geneva
In association with: P. Andrey, J.J. Oberson, L. Chenu, G. Descombes

Based on the idea of the brain as the central ethical and scientific pillar of the 21st century, the project inserts itself into the surrounding farmland and proposes a vision which unites the architecture of large spans with gardens and nature.

/ Der Entwurf kreist um das Thema Gehirn als objekthaftes Zeichen für das, was ethisch und wissenschaftlich im 21. Jahrhundert auf dem Spiel steht. Er bindet sich in eine ländliche Gegend ein und zeigt die Möglichkeit einer Allianz auf zwischen einer Architektur großen Maßstabs, Gartenanlagen und der freien Natur.

Lettre ouverte aux Suisses à propos d'une ville éphémère, Groupe des 30, Edition Zoé, Geneva, 1994

45. Headquarters of the European Union of Football / Verwaltungssitz der Europäischen Fußballunion

Competition, 2nd prize: 1994, commission for preliminary study: 1994, Route de Lac, Nyon, VD

The administrative headquarters of the UEFA, builds a terrace, or belvedere on which the building inserts itself in the manner of a large patrician house, overlooking the lake. The courtyards, patios and skylights bring light into the depths of the building and afford lateral views of the surrounding countryside. The facades alternate transparence (glass), translucence (marble or alabaster panels), and opacity (stone), in order to confront the strong interiority of the building with measured views of the landscape.

/ Der Entwurf sieht eine große Aussichtsterrasse vor, auf der das Administrationsgebäude der UEFA im Stile der am Genfersee üblichen großen Patrizierhäuser thront. Höfe, Patios und Oberlichter lassen auch im tiefen Innern des Baukörpers Helligkeit entstehen und geben Seitenblicke auf die Landschaft frei. An den Fassaden alternieren Transparenz (Glas), milchig durchscheinendes Licht (Marmor oder Alabasterplatten) und Lichtundurchlässigkeit (Stein) und spielen den starken Innenraumzusammenhalt gegen wohlbemessene Ausblicke auf die Landschaft aus.

SI + A, no. 43, 9 June 1994
Aktuelle Wettbewerbs Scene no. 4/5, July 1994
L'Hebdo, no. 3, 19–25 January 1995
AMC – Le Moniteur no. 10, October 1994

45.1 View of the building from the esplanade
45.2 Model (GF)
45.3 Plan of the entrance level on the esplanade

45.1

45.2

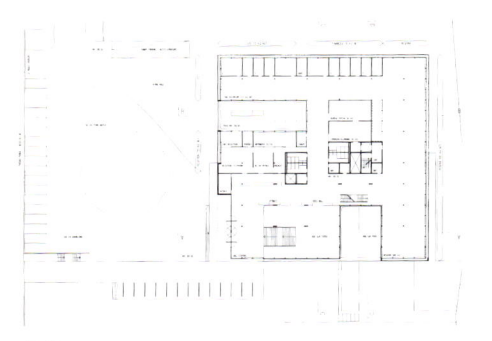

45.3

46. Transformation of a rural house / Umwandlung eines Landhauses

Built: 1995, Versonnex, Ferney-Voltaire, Ain
Collaborator: Laurent Matthey

47. New facades on the Place du Cirque / Fassadenerneuerung an der Place du Cirque

Project: 1995, built 1996, Place du Cirque 2–4, Geneva
Collaborators: Mylène Ducrey and François de Marignac

48. A social housing building / Staatlich subventionierte Wohnbauten

Commission for a preliminary study: 1995, Société Coopérative d'habitations de Lausanne, Ecublens VD

Placed in a garden, two houses whose plans make liberal use of oblique geometry to achieve sculptural, dimensional and functional aims.

/ Zwei in einen Park gesetzte Häuser, bei denen großzügig mit Schräggeometrien gearbeitet wurde, um plastische Wirkung, Gliederung und Funktionalität zu erzielen.

99

49. A psychiatric clinic / Psychiatrische Klinik

Competition: 1995, built 1996–, Centre de traitement psychiatriques du Nord Vaudois, Avenue des Sports, Yverdon, VD

49.3

A large semi-urban house, which references hotel or guesthouse buildings, regroups the pyschiatric clinic and the main day-clinic on an industrial site close to the centre of Yverdon. The project unites the traditional (every space is a room, the windows are vertical, etc.) with the solidity of its expression (brick, thick walls) around a courtyard garden open to the south.

/ Psychatrische Klinik und ambulante Station sind zusammen in einem großen Haus halburbanen Charakters untergebracht, dessen Gestaltung an ein Hotel oder eine Pension erinnert und das sich auf einem ehemaligen Industriegrundstück nahe dem Zentrum von Yverdon befindet. Der Entwurf greift Traditionelles auf (jeder Raum ist eine Zelle, das Fenster ist senkrecht usw.) und besteht auf Solidität (Ziegel, dicke Mauern). Zugleich entsteht räumliche Großzügigkeit mit dem nach Süden geöffneten Hofgarten.

49.1 View of the courtyard entrance
49.2 Plan of a level with psychiatric divisions
49.3 South facade

49.1

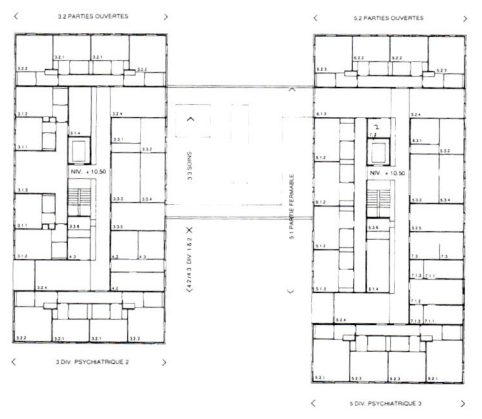

49.2

50. A theater in Neuchâtel / Theater in Neuchâtel

Competition, 5th prize, 1995, Passage Max-de-Meuron, Neuchâtel

'Place à la scène' is the project for a theater in a rear courtyard of the city; its only sign is the stage tower, a volume at once mysterious and representative.

/ «Platz für die Bühne» ist das Projekt eines Theaters im Hinterhof, dessen einziges Erkennungszeichen sein Bühnenturm mit Schnürboden wäre, ein ebenso mysteriöser wie repräsentativer Körper.

51. Gustave Doret district / Wohnviertel Gustave Doret

Competition, 1st rank and complementary study: 1995; Quai G. Doret, Lutry, VD
Collaborators: Hiéronyme Lacroix and Laurent Matthey

Between the buildings on the main street of Lutry and the edge of the lake is a district of low roofs, dense, with courtyards, narrow streets and patios. The response to the historic situation and unique character of the site is an apartment plan designed upon the premise of transparence in depth.

/ Ein dichtes und niedrig gehaltenes Viertel mit Höfen, Gassen und Patios, gelegen zwischen den Häusern der Hauptstraße von Lutry und dem Seeufer. Aus Rücksichtnahme auf die historische Architektur und den besonderen Charakter des Orts sind die Wohnungen so konzipiert, daß sie bei aller Tiefe immer noch einen trasparenten Charakter haben.

51.1 Site plan
51.2 Plan: lakeside apartment type

52. Villa Adlung / Villa Adlung

Built: 1996–97, Chemin des Grands-Prés, Tannay, VD
Collaborator: Olivier Andreotti

Under a large slate roof, which projects beyond the facades, is an apartment for two people. Its construction of painted plywood and standardised panelling contributes to the economy of the transparent shelter.

/ Unter einem großen Schieferdach mit weiten Auskragungen befindet sich ein Wohnraum für zwei Personen. Daß gestrichenes Schichtholz für die Konstruktion verwendet wurde und die Bauplatten Standardabmessungen haben, trägt zur Wirtschaftlichkeit des transparenten Unterschlupfs bei.

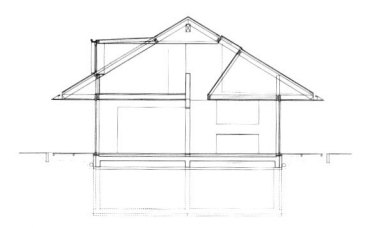

52.1 Transverse section
52.2 Plan

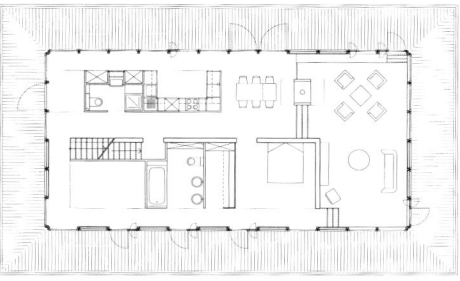

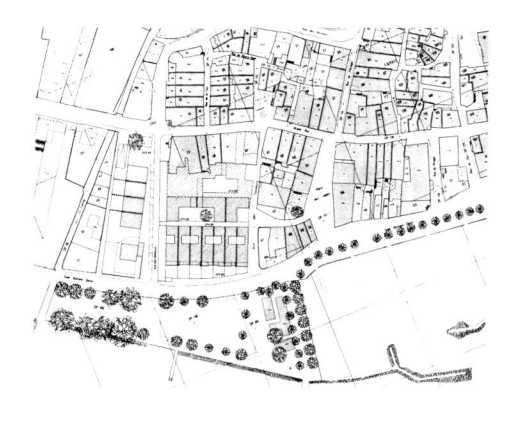

52.1

52.2

51.1

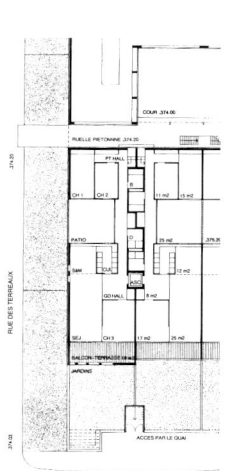

51.2

53. Exhibition 'four examples' / Ausstellung «four examples»

1996, Architekturgalerie Luzern

53.1 Plan of the exhibition

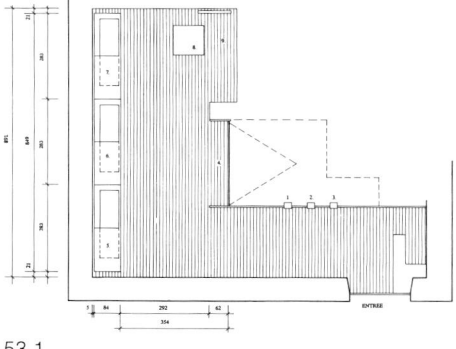

53.1

101

Wir danken

Toni Häfliger und Heinz Wirz von der Architekturgalerie Luzern für ihre Initiative und ihr Verständnis; Jo Abram für seinen Einleitungstext und seine wertvollen Bemerkungen. Jacques Gubler, dem stillen Beobachter; dem Graphiker Dominique Emmenegger für seine geduldige Arbeit und stete Symphatie, Fausto Pluchinotta für seine Photos von Grand-Saconnex, Pully und Cugy; Studio Page für die Ansichten der Aula von Lausanne; dem Videospezialisten Sergio Cavero und Marc Schwarz für die in der Ausstellung gezeigten Videos; für die Übersetzung Edmund Jephcott (deutsch) und Ingrid Taylor (englisch) sowie für das Lektorat Ursula Suter und Barry Stanton; und schließlich danken wir auch unseren Kunden für ihre engagierte Unterstützung und ihr Vertrauen. Ohne sie wäre überhaupt nichts möglich.

Des weiteren sei den folgenden Unternehmen gedankt, gleichzeitig für ihre fachliche Mitarbeit auf den Baustellen und ihre Unterstützung des Katalogs:

Bâtimétal SA, Construction métallique et serrurerie, Valeyres sur Montagny, Waadt
Delessert & Schiesser, Serrurerie et vitrerie, Puidoux et Belmont, Waadt
Dentan Frères, Maçonnerie et béton armé, Lausanne
Eberspächer AG, Metallbau, Glasbautechnik, Affoltern a. Albis
Eggly SA, Revêtement de sols, Genf
Elément SA, Préfabrication béton armé, Vernier, Genf
Fleury & Hollenstein, Plâtrerie et peinture, Bellevue, Genf
Griesser SA, protections solaires, Genf
Module 7, Mobilier, Lausanne
Norba SA, Menuiserie, Genf

Acknowledgments

We should like to express our thanks to Toni Häfliger and Heinz Wirz of the Architekturgalerie in Lucerne for their initiative and understanding. Also to Jo Abram for his introductory text and his precious questions. To Jacques Gubler, the discreet lifelong witness. Thanks, too, to the graphic artist, Dominique Emmenegger, for his patient research and his kind support. To Fausto Pluchinotta for his photographs of Grand-Saconnex, Pully and Cugy; and to Studio Page for the views of the EPFL lecture hall in Lausanne. To the video artists Sergio Cavero and Marc Schwarz for the videos presented at the exhibition. Also to the translators, Edmund Jephcott (German) and Ingrid Taylor (English) and to the readers Ursula Suter and Barry Stanton. Finally, to our clients, without whose enthusiasm and understanding none of this would have been possible.

In addition, we should like to express our thanks to the following companies for their knowledge of our constructions and their support in producing this catalogue:

Bâtimétal SA, Construction métallique et serrurerie, Valeyres sur Montagny, Vaud
Delessert & Schiesser, Serrurerie et vitrerie, Puidoux et Belmont, Vaud
Dentan Frères, Maçonnerie et béton armé, Lausanne
Eberspächer AG, Metallbau, Glasbautechnik, Affoltern a. Albis
Eggly SA, Revêtement de sols, Geneva
Elément SA, Préfabrication béton armé, Vernier, Geneva
Fleury & Hollenstein, Plâtrerie et peinture, Bellevue, Geneva
Griesser SA, protections solaires, Geneva
Module 7, Mobilier, Lausanne
Norba SA, Menuiserie, Geneva